To Al for his strength, and for my long-suffering family whose love has now put me on the right path.

Neil Thomas

THE ODD-JOB MAN

No Time to Die

AUSTIN MACAULEY PUBLISHERS™

LONDON • CAMBRIDGE • NEW YORK • SHARJAH

A CIP catalogue record for this title is available from the British Library.

ISBN 9781528997713 (Paperback)
ISBN 9781528997720 (ePub e-book)

www.austinmacauley.com

First Published (2021)
Austin Macauley Publishers Ltd
25 Canada Square
Canary Wharf
London
E14 5LQ

To my daughter, Lucy, who helped me turn the darkness into light.

This is a factual account; some names have been omitted for legal and security reasons.

It has taken well over 25 years for me to sit down and write this story. The reason for 'not' writing it until now is as the above. However, some of those limitations have now lapsed.

The reasons 'for' writing it now, I hope, will become apparent at the end of this story.

To those who have tried to take me down.
Revenge *est un plat qui se mange froid.*

Prologue

On the 25th of February 1980, the democratic government of the then five-year old Republic of Suriname was overthrown in a military *coup d'état*. The country had been granted independence in 1975 from Holland, but the public discontent with the fledgling government had forced a takeover.

The coup was instigated and led by 16 senior non-commissioned officers, headed by the dictator to be, Sergeant Desi Bouterse. At the time the public were completely behind the Sergeant's coup, but the years of murder, tyranny and corruption under Bouterse, would soon take their toll, on the people's confidence.

In March 1982, a countercoup was attempted, led by one, Wilfred Hawker, one of the Sergeants involved in the original takeover. This however was to fail and the luckless Hawker, injured in the fighting, was dragged from an operating table and executed by Bouterse's police. As were all his fellow conspirators.

In the latter half of 82, discontent with the military regime, increased among the population. An open confrontation with the military came about, with the support of four major trade unions, The 'Moeder bond'. The trade unions ordered a general strike, to try and force the military authority, into restoring democratic civilian rule.

On the 4th of November, Bouterse declared that an agreement had been reached with the protesters and the strike was called off.

However, this was just a ploy and on the 8th of December at around 2 o'clock in the morning, a number of people in the capitol Paramaribo, were taken from their beds and arrested. They were placed in front of a military tribunal, on charges of treason and the following day, they were executed. There would be no more strikes.

Disappearance's and summary executions, were to be the norm in the following years, as the people were terrorised into obedience.

The Maroon's (Bush Negroes), were treated with particular distrust by the dictatorship.

This and an argument over wages prompted the desertion in mid-1985 of one of Bouterse's bodyguards.

Ronnie Brunswijk, (a Cuban trained paratrooper from the east Suriname village of Moengo Tapoe), took refuge in the jungle and with the rising support of the population, began to fight back. He assumed the role of 'Robin Hood', robbing banks and army convoys then, distributing the gains to the local population.

With the growing support of the Maroon population, his activities quickly gained political dimensions and in 1986 he decided to turn his actions into a guerrilla war.

He proclaimed that he was fighting for democratic rule, for all the ethnic groups in Suriname.

He had no problem getting Maroon fighters to join him and he now began to get logistical support from exiled Surinamese people back in Holland.

Brunswijk named his rag-tag bunch of poorly armed and poorly trained Maroons, The Jungle Commando, (JC). Or even more optimistically, The Suriname National Liberation Army, (SNLA).

The JC, then went onto grow and over the following months, began to replace their shotguns and hunting rifles, with weapons captured from government soldiers. They also began receiving shipments of weapons from outside the country. The biggest triumph was to take down one of Bouterse's helicopters, that comprised of his air force, but other than that, fighting was minimal as were casualties.

Then on 29th November 1986, Bouterse sent a unit of soldiers by two helicopters, to the Bush village of Mooriwana. They indiscriminately murdered 35 men women and even children and burnt it to the ground. The 'unit' was discovered to be a force of Libyan 'Technical Advisers' and there was an international outcry over the massacre.

Something had to be done, quick, so Brunswijk called for the help of British Mercenaries to help in the fight. An organisation in Holland, calling themselves the Ansus Foundation, took on the task of recruitment. They had limited success and only managed to hire three, very dubious former soldiers. The three went to Suriname, but things did not go as well as planned. The JC quickly realising that they were not worth the money, sent them home.

However, peace talks were planned and a truce was made, but Bouterse still had other things up his sleeve. He began arming the Tucajanas, these are the indigenous Amer-Indians of the country and the whole of that part of South America.

There was racial hatred between the Bush blacks and the Tuc and this was something that he could now capitalise on. Now as a separate war began, it was clear that the peace possess was a sham and again something had to be done, to turn the tide.

Talks began again about outside help, to train not just the JC, but now large numbers of other disillusioned volunteers, over in the west of the country.

The only person they knew from 1986/7, who they thought had actually been a soldier, was a man called John. In 1989, they begrudgingly called him again and told him this time, they needed real soldiers and more of them.

Chapter 1

Suriname, South America.
09 December 1989

The ambush was set.

In the dark, I lay down against a fallen tree in silence, watching.

The tree must have fallen only recently, since some of the leaves were still clinging to life on its branches. It wouldn't be long before it began to decay, and millions of insects began to infest it, helping the process. The usual array of them were still crawling about their business, but in the time, I had been here, I had learned to ignore them, as they had, me.

The mozzies – so vicious at the beginning of my time here also seemed to be leaving me alone, these days. I put it down to the remedies given to me by the locals and the fact that I now stank like the jungle itself.

As always at this time of the year, and in this part of the world, it was almost unbearably hot and humid but like the insects, my body was beginning to adapt and acclimatise to the conditions. The climate almost felt comfortable now, as I melted into my surroundings.

I looked across to Al in the main fireteam. I couldn't really see his face in the darkness under the jungle canopy, but I could tell him by his outline and the shape of the Minimi LMG (light machine gun) he was resting on a mound in front of him. Another former royal marine, Al was one of the reasons I had ended up here in the first place. One of the most genuine, trustworthy men I have ever met. As I looked over, I had a little smile to myself. Even though I couldn't see the fag hanging out of the side of his mouth, I knew it would be there – unlit, of course.

Further across, way over to my right, was Bill (the professor) with the other cut-off team. Bill was a former French Foreign Legionnaire, and didn't really look the rough, tough, soldier type, but he had been more of an asset on this job than any Boot-neck, (marine), Para (paratrooper) or Blade (SAS) I have ever known. My eyes strained in the darkness and although I couldn't see him, I knew he was there, like me, rifle in hand, silently waiting.

There were just three of us left, now, from the team of eight that had made the journey.

One, a complete fantasist – a 'Walter Mitty' – had gone back to England after two days, quickly realising just how out of his depth he was.

Another had been shot dead, and three others had been disarmed at gunpoint and escorted back to French Guiana, very lucky to leave with their lives.

So here we were, the three effing Musketeers, still stuck in this war-torn shit-hole, trying to clear up the mess.

More than twenty men had been gathered from the so-called JC (Jungle Commando). Men we had been trying to train into some sort of organised unit, for the last few months.

We put them into three different teams and did some quick, dry ambush drills, then set them out with me as the left cut-off group, Al in the centre with two LMGs (light machine guns) in the main fire team, and Bill to the right, with the other cut-offs. We had the three youngest as (very relieved) spares: one to stay with the transport at the drop-off point and two in the final RV, (rendezvous) as rear cover.

It was all very basic – time was running short and we didn't want to confuse them.

Earlier, Castro, the second-in-command of the JC, had burst into our room at the main base of the YMCA building in Moengo, demanding,

"You must come! Many Tuc are coming! You have to go to kill them! Now!"

The Tuc – Tucayana – were the JC's most hated enemy (it was a racial thing) and we had already been on the receiving end of what they could dish out. However, with all that had happened prior to this, I really didn't give a shit what Castro wanted. I didn't like the vicious bastard, anyway. Before we did anything else, I needed to talk to the organ grinder.

"Get me Ronnie, now!" I said.

The JC Leader, Ronnie, came to me to sort things out. He knew what the problem was, but again, he went through the same bullshit process of asking.

We had taken the job as a training team some months before, on the promise of payment, and had seen very little of the folding stuff, so far. Now, the word 'mercenary' might spring to mind, and in the world of those who believe what's written in Soldier of Fortune magazine a bit too much, that may be – but not with me. I was technically here as an instructor, and I had my reasons to keep it like that. Yes, the boundaries had been blurred a few times, and we had acted accordingly to save our arses and the lives of others. However, I tried to clear those blurred lines as best I could and stick to the task I'd been given.

Now, though, through no fault of mine or the rest of my team, the whole situation was escalating into war. And I wasn't risking our lives for peanuts any more.

Ronnie could see that we were rock solid on the issue, but because he was panicked by the approaching Tuc, he begged, "Please! You must go! This must all be stopped by you, now!"

He was trying to put pressure on us, for something that had happened earlier.

"What happened before," I said, calmly, "had nothing to do with us and you know it." It had, in fact, been partly his fault – and we were not moving.

He then shoved some local money in our hands – a fortune to the people here, but worth nothing in the real world.

We just stared at him until, reluctantly, he shouted, "Okay. Okay!" and sent someone to bring his special bag.

Five minutes later, a black backpack arrived and he passed it to us. I asked Bill to look, and as he opened it, I caught sight of bundles of French francs and Dutch guilders. It looked promising, but after Bill quickly counted it, he shook his head. It was nowhere near enough.

I looked again to Ronnie, who was now pleading with us, promising us more on our return.

I had my own reasons to go and deal with this, but it was wrong to expect Al and Bill to join me. However, by now, we all had people we really liked, living in this area and we had seen the sickening aftermath of who we thought were Tuc and what they had done to civilians, too many times. If they actually made it to Moengo, en masse, it wouldn't be pleasant for anyone.

I looked questioningly at Al and Bill and knowing this, with a nod they agreed, to one last Op.

The Jungle drums (local radio communication) were telling us that the Tuc were coming from the north, on the main tarmacked road. There were up to a hundred of them. We had to move quickly, so now, along with Castro and the other JCs, we jumped into the various flat-backed trucks and headed out of Moengo. Normally, Castro, like Ronnie, would avoid any kind of combat, but prior to this, what had happened with others in the team had caused 'all hell' to break loose.

So now, much to Castro's annoyance, Ronnie wanted him to keep a beady eye on us.

As we jumped into the various vehicles, I looked at the volunteers around us. Most of them were of Bush Negro Maroon descent and the biggest bunch of misfits you would ever meet. Some really did believe in the cause they were fighting for, but a lot were just murderers, rapists and thieves – on the run, and here only because they had nowhere else to go. All, as usual, were dressed like Rambo, with the customary bandanas and linked rounds of ammo across their shoulders. Looking the part, but I could see in their eyes – volunteers they were not. Only Madman, the exiled Cuban, seemed to be up for a firefight and, as in the times before, I was glad he was with us.

My mind now raced, while the trucks sped north. Something had always bothered me about the radio info we got from the various spotters in the surrounding villages.

Nothing was clear-cut here, and I knew that for any info we had on the Tuc, you can bet they had more on us.

It had been raining and, as always, the heat was stifling. It felt good to be speeding along in the back of the open truck, having the night air wash around me; but this was no time to relax and I kept my eyes focused firmly on the treeline.

Then, way before the place where Castro had wanted us to drive, I saw the point I was looking for. Banging on the roof of the lead truck, I shouted, "Stop! Stop here, now!"

As we slowed down, I jumped out and ordered the confused JC to conceal the vehicles off the road. The boys knew what was happening and both of them, with Madman, immediately made for the gap in the trees, to recce (reconnoitre).

Then, with the trucks hidden off the road and one of the 'kids' left behind, we moved off.

Now, much to the annoyance of Castro and the rest of the JC, we were going on foot for the last few kilometres – through the bush. By now, I knew this area a little, from the many patrols we had made with the JC, teaching them the basic skills of spacing – and the direction each should point their rifle. It had also helped us to secure the area for local JC sympathisers and they were the ones who had shown us this shortcut, with a defined track through to the location where I wanted to set the ambush. The slightly clearer track still didn't stop the JC whinging about having to walk through the bush. So, with Bill as point man, Al and Madman went to the back to make sure none of the 'volunteers' sloped off.

For a chubby bugger, Bill moved well – and stealthily making his way along, he stopped a few hundred metres from the ambush site, signalling to the final RV. We left the other two 'kids' to man it, checking they knew the signal for our return and moved off in slow, slow, time, keeping as quiet as you can in the jungle. Those who have been there know how difficult it is to move quietly through mainly secondary jungle with a large force. Along with the sounds of the displacement of vegetation, the various creatures can smell and hear you coming a mile off, so they give you away – and at night, it's even worse.

Bill, though, was on it, and like some kind of Crocodile Dundee, he stopped regularly just to listen to the sounds of the jungle, and I swear I could see him sniffing the air. We were off to *set* an ambush and Bill had no intention of walking us into one.

I was thankful for the track and we made ground reasonably easily. Bill then made his final stop, before a break in the trees, where the road wound round to our right. This was it.

Al quietly set out his team in a line with Castro, where they would have good arcs of fire and he ran out the three homemade Claymores – (directional explosives) – Professor Bill had knocked up, while I went off to the right with Bill and his team, to do the same.

Once Bill was happy with his position, I went back to Al and picked up my group waiting with Madman.

As I had done with Bill, I whispered to Al, "Watch your back, mate."

He gave me that knowing look, then me and my team moved off to the left.

This was a bad time for us, since we were now split up, and in the dark, with way more of the JC around us than we were now comfortable with. A bullet could come from anywhere. Therefore, like the Navy Seals in Vietnam, we had a code word.

The Seals, like us, had trained locals against the VC, but they could turn on them and had done so, many times. Knowing this, the Seals came up with a plan to kill the people around them, if it all went tits up (bad). They would make up an obscure code word and if someone shouted it, they would start blasting everyone around them.

In fact, we had a double code word: Duran, Duran. Yes, I know, seems funny when you think about it now – and it even was, at the time, but it just came up in the conversation and I was a big fan. With Duran, Duran, going through my head, giving Madman a wink, I set my team down.

The main instruction we had tried to ram down the JC's throats was to just stay completely still and quiet. No one was to open fire until me, Al or Bill gave a signal – by voice, or by opening fire.

I looked out across the road. It was a good spot. The trees had been felled ready for farming over the other side, and the moon lit the road up well. All we had to do now was wait. So, I did just that, silently leaning against that fallen tree.

I had lain in many ambushes and OPs (observation posts) before – mostly on training exercises, but some in real life, during the Falklands War and what was then the Badlands of South Armagh in Northern Ireland. You would lie uncomfortably – mostly cold and wet – for hours, even days. All for nothing.

Now, within an hour, I could hear something coming from the road, to my left. I tilted my ear towards the direction of the sound and opened my jaw slightly, a little trick I had been taught by an old sweat instructor many years before, as a young recruit at Commando Training Centre, RM (Royal Marines). Opening the jaw slightly helps to amplify sound. Sounds like bullshit – but in this environment, it worked really well, and I could now make out noises that did not match the normal jungle hum. My eyes were now peeled wide open.

Out in the distance, under the grey light of the moon, I could see a shadowy group of what looked like heavily armed men headed towards us. I had expected them to come through at speed, in vehicles, but surprisingly, they were all on foot.

The small number of shit radios we had were open mike, so they were switched off. I gave a subtle 'hiss-hiss' to Al who passed it on to Bill. This was the signal that things were about to go live.

There were about forty of them, and not the number given on the drums. This was better odds, but it was still about two to one, against. They were spread over a large area, casually smoking and walking with their guns down by their sides or draped over the shoulder. My idea of dropping the vehicles early seemed to have worked. If they had been warned, I would have expected them to be on full alert. But here they were now, without a clue about all the eyes following them.

There was no fear now. Having already been through what we had endured, I was way past that. I did, however, still have deep concerns. Not about the people out on the road, but about the people lying next to me. Apart from the constant threat that one would just shoot me in the back, I thought they might just jump up and simply run away or let loose a shot at the wrong time.

Thankfully, they all held off on slotting (killing) us and kept their nerve.

As I continued to watch the enemy get closer, I could now clearly see their faces in the moonlight. The descriptions of the Tucayana – the indigenous Amer-Indian people of South America and ruthless jungle fighters that the bush negro JC hated with a passion – again, were not evident, here. The people in my rifle sights right now were no different from the JC. Just another rag-tag group, working for a different paymaster. Some, to my mind, way too young to be there at all.

I wiped those thoughts from my head, because it didn't matter, now. Whoever they were, there was a bigger picture here, and I knew what had to be done.

They were strewn out for quite a distance, but the majority had moved right where we wanted them: straight in front of Al's killing group.

As I scanned across the faces through the sights of my rifle, ignoring the sweat now running heavily over my eyes, I picked out someone who looked as if he had some authority, and got a lock.

My mouth went dry and time seemed to stand still. I thought for a millisecond about what we were about to do; then the training I had been given over the years took over and as if on automatic pilot, I tightened my finger around the trigger and squeezed.

As my rifle cracked into life, I saw my first round make contact. The guy spun as it hit him and the back of his shoulder exploded before he slumped to the ground. Then, I heard a long volley of machine gun fire to my right. It was Al, who had taken his own cue and opened up at almost exactly the same time as me.

Some of the JC then followed suit. However, a lot of them had yet to take their safety catches off or were fucking about trying to get their weapons to work. As they did, the volume of fire quickly increased and then, when the claymores went off, the whole jungle seemed to shake.

Half a dozen of the Tuc were shredded instantly, but some managed to hit the deck, so I tried to pick them off as they crawled toward the bush for cover. Others scattered everywhere and a couple even charged directly towards Al's killing group. The two machine guns just ripped them to pieces.

Then, a number of the JC – who had probably been chewing on the drugs they were so fond of – jumped up, screaming, and ran towards the track. Al tried to stop them, but more of them did just did the same. In the spur of the moment, me, Bill and Al followed on, firing and manoeuvring towards the road, trying to take as many of the escaping Tuc as we could. Then, one of the claymores that hadn't yet been set off blew, – and almost took out a couple of JC who had made it to the track.

It was fucking carnage.

The three of us regrouped at the edge of the track, and I tried to get Castro to calm his men down, because rounds were still going everywhere. But he, too, seemed beyond listening. Meanwhile, the JC started mutilating the bodies on the floor and rifling through their pockets.

As I looked around at the blood spilling out across the moonlit road, I told Castro, "That's us, done. We want no part of this now."

His eyes were glazed as I spoke, but he nodded his understanding.

"We'll meet you back at the RV," I said.

Then, after a final glance at what we had done, with Madman in tow, the four of us made off.

Once back at the RV, with the smell of cordite (gunpowder residue) and PE (plastic explosive) still heavy in my nose, we sat and contemplated what had just happened. It hadn't seemed real. It was all too easy – what the Yanks would call a 'turkey shoot'.

I could still see the all their faces as they were taken out.

There was no 'right' side, here. Ronnie and his men were no different to the people we had just killed. By now, we knew that Ronnie was running a big drugs operation, with flights going out on a weekly basis. That's all that seemed to be going on, here – battling over who controlled the drugs. The intelligence teams working in the area knew this; but that was okay, because, for now, Ronnie was their man.

I looked at the faces around me. I could see a change in all of us, now. We looked older than we should, and very, very tired. The three adventurers who had started this were now three cold, heartless bastards.

I began to boil inside, thinking about the two arseholes who had put us in this no-win situation. We had come as a training team but were now killing for money in some glorified giant gang war. And as unbelievable as it may sound and even as I write this I cannot get my head around it. I still hadn't quite reached my 25th birthday.

We sat for what seemed like hours hearing the odd gunshot and screams that I tried to blank out, before the JC trickled back. We hoped they'd all calmed down enough, now, so there would be no trouble between us and them.

Castro was absolutely full of himself, as if he'd taken the Tuc on singlehanded. However, he addressed us with a respect that hadn't been there before, and asked us, "What should we do, now?"

We told him that we had to move back to the trucks as quickly as possible, which he ordered his men to do.

We were slow, moving back, unbelievably none of the JC had been killed but some of them were injured – mostly from accidentally shooting each other, I thought. Others were weighed down with extra weapons and anything else they had managed to steal.

We began loading up in the trucks, but testosterone and drugs still filled the air. The JC were still very volatile and I looked around, thinking that if anybody looked at me the wrong way, Duran, Duran were ready to sing, and I was ready to blow everyone's fucking head off.

As we drove off, back towards Moengo, things seemed to settle a little. A couple of them even patted me on the back, and one said, in his heavy bush accent, "That was good. That was good."

We rattled along in the back of the truck, and I was enjoying the comfort of the night air around me again, but all I could think about, now, was getting the hell out of there and going back home.

We got back to Moengo and the YMCA without a hitch, where Ronnie was waiting to greet everyone.

As we jumped off the trucks, there was lots of shaking of hands and hugging, and Ronnie was just full of praise for me, and the boys. The mood was cheerful and celebratory. Beers were then passed around, while the JC started re-enacting their parts in the ambush, chattering loudly, animated. Even though I couldn't understand what they were saying, I knew that this story was already being inflated.

Now, with all the banter and laughter, we felt a bit more comfortable and began to try to enjoy the moment. More beer came, and we had calmed down a little, when we spotted Castro having a serious chin wag with Ronnie. Something was up, so I bowled straight up to them and asked what was going on.

Ronnie just gave me his one of his big warm smiles and said, "It's okay. No problem. We have to do something, now, but you go inside and relax."

Still a little suspicious, we did what he asked and went into the dining area to see if we could find some food.

About ten minutes later, one of the local teenagers who tried to hang around with the JC came in and shouted, "Ronnie wants to see you back outside!" Then, he ran off.

We stepped out of the front door but couldn't see anyone, so with fingers on triggers we walked down to the end of the building.

Then, as we carefully rounded the corner, the JC opened fire.

Chapter 2

London. Early August, 1989

We were running late. Rich Arabs are never on time for anything. So, things were pretty normal as we continued to break the speed limit along the M4 towards Heathrow.

The Sheik, his wife and their new-born baby girl were in the lead limo with Darcy, and I was in the follow-up, with Mick, the wife's main Filipino maid, and some of the luggage. The rest of the many bags and a couple more maids were in a people-carrier behind us. I could see the driver in the rear-view mirror, struggling like hell to keep up.

We turned off – not into the main entrance to the terminals, but the way the very rich avoid customs altogether and board their private jets. The security guard waved us straight through the open gate, since he had already been given the diplomatic licence plate number and been told to let it through, along with any vehicles accompanying it.

The term 'private jet' may suggest a small, sleek thing. Well, not the one we were approaching. It was a Boeing 747. We pulled up to the steps already in place and we could see the ground staff pacing around, stressed.

Now, the Sheik had some pull, but not enough to start messing with the allocated time slots at Heathrow. So, he and his wife, along with the baby, made a quick exit from the limo and up the stairs to board.

Now for the entertainment.

Arabs are not the most organised of people in the world – but throw in some Filipino maids, and piss-up and brewery come to mind.

Darcy shouted, "Here we fucking go!" as the arms went up and the squabbling began.

As normal, the security team and drivers all ignored the chaos, grabbed any bag they could, and started up the stairs to load them onto the plane.

Now, you can ignore all the bullshit about being a bodyguard you have seen on TV. Even the American Secret Service end up lugging suitcases in and out of vehicles. Trust me – I know. Later in life, I ended up working with an ex-Agent and when he'd had a few sherbets, he would go on and on about how unbelievably boring it had been. And he used the term 'baggage-handler' quite a lot.

While I am on the subject, I need to shed a little reality on the firearm situation for civilian close protection teams in Britain. Apart from members of internationally recognised organisations like the Secret Service, the only people on the UK mainland who could carry concealed firearms for close protection at that time were The Diplomatic Protection Group, The Royal Protection Team and Special Branch. All are police, with a warrant card and a concealed weapons ticket.

So, if some fat ex-Army guy down the pub starts telling you he carries a weapon because he looks after a pop star – tell him to jog on. The number of Walters on the security circuit going for imaginary shooters under their jackets after a car backfires is unreal.

Having said that, as well as selected SF (Special Forces) military units, there were two civilian firms at that time who, under exceptional circumstances, could get authorisation from the British Government to carry firearms, (as with Salman Rushdie). I could give their names, but I am not going to – and at that time, I was working for neither.

Now, moving on to the less conventional carrying of *un*registered firearms. There was, on occasion, a pistol available. However, this was kept in cars with diplomatic plates only, and was generally brought with the Principal when they arrived. This was then placed into the glove box of the car and that's where it stayed – only to be pulled out in extreme circumstances.

As Mick and I lifted and shifted the bags, Darcy was placing a 9 mm Browning (old-school) and two full mags from the car into a bag, then he carried it up the stairs to the plane. Inside, there was a safe for it and Darcy was just popping it in there as we were heaving the last of the bags on.

There was another reason for us all being so helpful – we hadn't had our customary bung (Bonus) yet; so, we tried to hang around in the aircraft for as long as possible.

Now, normally – in its usual configuration – this aircraft could carry a few hundred passengers, but here, it was fitted out for no more than a dozen. The space was made up of a huge master bedroom with on suite, a cinema with two rows of big recliner chairs, a kitchen with dining table and some smaller rooms that I didn't get a look into. This is the life of oil-rich Arabs. Meanwhile, we stood waiting, only wanting a tiny little piece as a thank you.

It came in its usual form – fat brown envelopes from the Sheik's Pakistani assistant, who had been waiting with the aircraft. He gave them to Darcy (senior security) to dish out and on seeing this transaction, we all retreated down the stairs.

The plane was now firing up to taxi, so Mick, Darcy and I jumped into the lead car with Marc, the driver, and we sped off, with the other vehicles following.

As soon as we were clear of the aircraft, Darcy pulled out his envelope and began counting.

When he had finished, he wasn't pleased.

"This is fucking *less* than *last* time!" he moaned and as he dished the rest out, he continued: (referring to the Pakistani assistant). "I bet that fucking thieving bastard has slipped a few in his own pocket!"

Darcy had a way with words.

Then, Mick, after counting his, joined in. "Fucking hell, man! This is fucking shit, man!"

Mick also had a way with words, 'man'.

Mick Pemberton was, in his mid-twenties and ex-military. He had just done five years in the French Foreign Legion's 2nd Rep (Paratroopers). I knew some of Mick's family back in my North East home, and friends of mine had married both his sisters. He had introduced me to the Close Protection circuit in London. Like Darcy, Mick was handy with his fists and easy to get along with, but unlike Darcy, he was what we would call 'bone' (Dumb).

He also elaborated on his time in the Legion just a little too much, for me. I knew from other Legionnaires I had spoken to and believed that out in North Africa, where Mick did his tours in the mid-eighties, all they did – in the words of Blackadder – was use assault rifles against people with sharp sticks. There was no fighting, as such. It was just the colonial French, protecting their interests. There were a few former

Legion who had done Beirut and some Falklands War vets out on the circuit, now – including me – and I think Mick was just trying to keep up with the Joneses.

I had been on this particular job for the last two months and had been told by Darcy that this one was a pretty good one, as working for the Arabs goes. I had been tasked with looking after the Sheik's new young wife. Out of professional curtesy, I won't name names. She was actually really nice and a pleasure to protect. Everything was new to her in London and she went around everywhere, all excited. Although I felt for her a little, because I knew it wouldn't be long before the shine washed off her life, as I had seen in the eyes of the other, older wives before her, who also lived in the same very large house. She had just had a baby girl – totally unimportant in an oil-rich Arab's life – but she clearly adored her.

Darcy, a big bruiser of a man, was looking after the Sheik who – because he was off whoring all the time – would generally send Darcy off with me, to keep an eye on the baby.

Kidnapping the children is very lucrative – rich Arabs tend not to involve the police; they pay as requested, then get their security services involved to hunt the kidnappers down. If they are caught, there is no trial. So, assigned to the wife and child, me and Darcy had a right old time at all the London attractions and theme parks. The best thing about looking after the ladies is that you're always back and on your way to the pub when the shops shut. To this day, I still have an expensive, Seiko divers watch that she bought me as a thank you.

I could tell you a lot of stories about some of the so-called royalty of the Arab States, but I have good reason not to. I had met a guy called Spider, who had been doing this sort of work since the late sixties/ early seventies. He was getting on a bit, by then, and dyed his hair to make himself look younger, but he knew his days doing this job were numbered, with all the young soldiers seeing an opportunity to make a bit more money than they did in the forces.

He had been keeping a detailed diary over the years, of all his time with various Arab families of high status. This was his 'out' – he reckoned he could profit from his stories and retire happily ever after. He was about to publish a book about what he's witnessed: all the whores and the drink and coke-filled parties that didn't tally with the public persona of these devout Muslims.

I never saw Spider again after that. Neither, it seems, did anyone else – not even any of his family. He had completely disappeared from the face of the earth and his book was never published.

That is why I will never kiss and tell on the Arabs. Well, maybe I would – when the oil is no longer the prime source of energy. Not long now, gentlemen! Not long, now.

With me thinking *I will never eat another McDonald's again!* we continued back towards central London. I was sitting in the back of the Limo with Mick, chatting and he was going on, again – about a job he might be doing in South America.

I was wanting out of the security circuit – already I could see it was a dead end. I had another path I was going down, but again, I humoured him. He was meeting the guy who was running the job that night – in a pub in Wimbledon.

"Why don't you come along, man?" Mick said he's looking for guys with previous combat experience.

I gave him the 'don't kid a kidder' look.

"Come on, man! Just a few beers and a chat. It'll be a laugh."

Again, I had heard too much bullshit on the security circuit to follow this up.

Then, however, he said, "There's another bloke coming. Works on the door. I think he knows you from 40 (Royal Marine Commando Unit). A guy called Al."

"Al?" I said, with interest.

I had left 40 just after Al joined. He was about the same age as me, but signed up a few years after I had. It was late in 1984 and most of the unit had done the Falklands war and had not long returned from an NI trip, where we had lost a good lad from B Coy. The unit was then prepping for a UN tour and with almost everyone else in 40 a seasoned soldier, Al was the sprog. That didn't bother him, though – he took it all in his stride. However, if anyone went too far, he wasn't afraid to lay into them. That's where he got his broken nose.

Mick described him – and since it sounded like the Al I knew, it would be good to catch up.

"Okay," I conceded. "I'm in!"

As we were dropped off, we set a time to meet up, then said our goodbyes to Darcy and all the drivers. "Till the next one!"

That evening, I stared up and down at myself in the mirror on the wall of the glorified bedsit I was renting. Even though I'd told Mick I wasn't really interested, I was still trying to get the right look for a job interview. *You never know.* I glared at the suit I was wearing, then thought, *Bollocks!* and switched to the usual desert boots, jeans and open-necked shirt. *Take me as I am,* I thought, picked up my keys and slammed the door behind me.

As I reached the door of the pub, there he was, in his penguin suit – Alan Boydell, just as I remembered him. Broken nose, a big grin on his face and always with a fag hanging out of the side of his mouth.

He spotted me and shouted in his slightly Janner accent: "Hello, mate! How yer doing?" Then he immediately tried to squeeze me to death.

"Alright, mate! Alright," I said, trying to get my breath back.

"Your mate Mick's through there." He pointed to some booths over in the corner. "I'll be over in a bit. Good to see yer."

"Likewise, Al, likewise," I said, as he manhandled a few people out of the way to give me a clear run.

Mick was sitting opposite two men. I sat down next to him and he introduced me, saying, "This is John and Pat. John's the one running the job."

John Richards was a little older than the rest of us – in his mid-thirties maybe, with a very worn face. Mick had told me John had been Legion 2nd Rep but had deserted after three years. His arms were littered with homemade tattoos and the stains on his fingers revealed his chain-smoking. If he had been an animal, I would have put him as the runt of the litter. Already, there was an air about him that I didn't like.

Pat Baker was in his mid to late 20s and seemed the complete opposite to John – a big, jolly lad, with a moon face. Pat smiled and shook my hand immediately. I went to shake John's, but he reluctantly put his hand out limply and almost ignored me.

OK, I thought, *If, that's how it is – that's how it is.*

For all that Pat was friendly and chatty, the military background he spoke of through the evening was sketchy and I had him tagged as a Walter straight away. However, he was really good company and sort of cracked the ice with everyone.

Later, Al came over to the booth and joined us with a load of beers. "On the house," he said and pushed himself in, next to me.

John then hunched forward, did the furtive 'I have something secret to tell' glance around, and proceeded to tell us all about the job.

He was looking for five soldiers to join him on a training mission to Suriname in South America.

At the time, none of us knew anything about Suriname, but John had worked there before. We were to go and train a rebel force – The Jungle Commando (JC) – who were against the ruling dictatorship of Desi Bouterse. This training was to begin in the east of the country, and after we'd given basic infantry skills to the JC, we were to move west, avoiding the heavily protected north around the capital, Paramaribo.

Once there, we were to meet up with members of the affluent western Asian population, the leaders of whom were part-funding the operation, because they were also keen to depose Bouterse and re-establish a more favourable government.

At the time, the JC had the fighting numbers, but limited money – whereas the population of the west were not fighters, but – we were told – had bundles of dosh.

Now all of this, to me, sitting there with my pint, was a bit of a bombshell – and as we listened, we each had a million questions. We held onto most of them for the moment, but not Al.

"How much?" he said, as soon as John took a breath.

John was a bit taken aback at first, but then, he told us, "£1000 expenses each, prior to leaving. And £30,000 once in country…"

A lot of expletives burst out from everyone, because back in 1989, for about three-four months, work – that was a hell of a lot of money.

As the night went on, more questions snuck out with each beer – although we trod lightly, not wanting to undermine John's authority and his previous time in Suriname. As I sat there, listening to all the answers he calmly gave, I just couldn't get my head round it. This one seemed so far-fetched; it could be true!

I was now in a bit of a dilemma. The other path I was pursuing was still going very slowly. This job was about to happen very soon – and it seemed a nice chunk of money to help me on my way. I didn't know what to think. I also didn't know what John thought of me and whether or not he would offer me the job, anyway.

Well, the beer kept on flowing till I stopped thinking too much – and I as left the pub, if nothing else came out of it, we all seemed to have had a good night.

The next day, the phone rang. It was one of those American types of phone – on the wall next to the fridge. With a bouncing headache, I jumped up and answered.

"Hello, Royal!" It was Al, sounding like he'd been on orange juice all night. I hadn't been a Royal for some time now, but never mind.

He told me John had offered us all the job and wanted to speak to us again. He also wanted to show us some film he had, of his time in Suriname, so Al invited me over to his then-girlfriend's flat in Wimbledon, for us all to meet again that afternoon.

"Roger that, mate," I said, "see you then."

But as soon as I put the phone down, alarm bells started ringing – and it wasn't the hangover.

This wasn't right. Offering a job like this to someone you'd just had a few drinks with down the pub, didn't sit well with me. I could go to my phonebook and get ten guys I'd worked with, who I knew could do this job with their eyes closed! Marines, Pathfinders, SAS, SBS… What the hell was going on, here? It went around and around in my head. Even though I liked Mick, he was just plain bone and would never have made my list. Pat was an obvious Walter. So, the only one I could see myself working with was Al. I just couldn't figure it.

As we say up north, John was a wrong 'un. What the hell was I going to do?

I sat, stumped for a while, then thought, *fuck it – let's see where this goes.*

Walking into Al's front room, through the haze of smoke I could already see some open beer cans. John was sitting in the chair opposite the TV, with the rest of the lads just lounging around.

"Here ya go, Royal." Al gave me a can, and I sat on the arm of the sofa.

"Al, while you're on your feet, can you get that couple of video cassettes from my bag?" John asked him. "And play them on the VCR."

"Sure." Al said as he padded across the room, swigging from his can.

"We were filmed by a French camera team while I was in Suriname, in late 1986," John explained while the first tape wound on. "Watch. You might learn something," he said arrogantly, taking another drag on his fag.

The films contained scenes of John and the other two members of his team working alongside the JC. The only dramatic moment in the videos was some footage of them destroying a bridge with plastic explosives. But John told us they had ambushed an Army truck, killing all inside and gave us various other combat stories.

The films were useful, in the fact that it showed us the area and the men we would be training. Anything else he said, I took with a pinch of salt.

I was even more conflicted now than I was before. It was clearly John in the videos, so you had to sort of believe what was going on here. Again, I said to myself, *Let's just see where this goes.*

For now, where it was going, was another piss-up. The drinks flowed and the banter started. It's just that way with soldiers, wherever they come from. It was, by then, into early evening and it wasn't going to stop there. Pat then told us about a nurse's club in Roehampton, near where he lived. That was our mission for the time being – so we upped sticks and headed over.

When we arrived, it was empty, all but for one bloke at the bar – and John headed straight over to him and started chatting. The man at the bar, Mick explained, was Bill – an old acquaintance of John's. They had met through the Legion's old boy network around London – and he was also coming on this job. Given that fact, I took a closer look at him: in his late 20s early 30s and a little overweight. Again, he looked an unlikely prospect.

John brought him over and introduced us. "Bill Oakey ex-Legion, like me, but not 2nd Rep Para. He was infantry/engineers…"

As John told it, Bill's military past, if true, was glamorous: he had served for three years, culminating in being shot in the head in Beirut in 1983. He was medically discharged, having been awarded the Croix de la Valour Militaire.

Again, I took it all with another pinch of salt, as I was introduced to him and shook his hand. That said, after we sat down and talked, it was obvious that he was unbelievably knowledgeable. He spoke three different languages fairly fluently and knew the technical details of any weapon I had ever heard of.

What I noticed most, though – apart from the fact that he looked like he would never pass a BFT (Battle Fitness Test), these days – was that he loved a drink and seemed to consume twice as much as any of us. I pulled him on it, in the nicest way.

"How the hell can you drink that much and not be on the floor?" I said, pleasantly.

"It's the bullet wound in my head…" he explained, tapping his forehead. "…damaged the nerves. So now, I don't get drunk."

I was running out of salt, now. But whatever I thought, I couldn't help but like Bill. He didn't take himself too seriously, and I could have sat sponging off his brain all night.

There were now a couple of ladies in the bar and Pat was moving in on them. He was a funny bugger and was charming them with a few jokes.

John however, then did the strangest thing and completely ruined anyone's chances. There was a large window that separated the bar from a gym below, where an aerobics class was going on. He pulled up a chair right in front of the glass, then sat and just stared at the women below, doing their exercises. Bill tried to get him back to the bar, but John thought he was hilarious and wouldn't budge. So, we just left him there, leering.

I sat back down with Bill, where he then began to tell me he had known John, and about the job, for quite some time. Maybe because of the drink – I don't know, but he then confided in me about John's previous operation in Suriname in 1986/7 – and how it wasn't quite the success John had made it out to be. Surprise, surprise.

John had answered an ad in the Soldier of Fortune magazine and had recruited only two others for the job. One of them was a former soldier – nobody knew which unit – and the other was a civilian. The latter had proved to be the more useful of the two, because the former soldier just got drunk every day; but the civilian was talented with explosives and allegedly had been a bit of a safebreaker. Bill told me the reason John was recruiting again was because the backers had stopped the money, due to John's – as Bill tactfully put it – 'lack of productivity'.

A little later in the evening, Mick's new French girlfriend, Katy, and her sister, Sophie, arrived. Mick had been telling us earlier in the evening what a great girl she was: "Yeah, man. Me and Katy, man. King and Queen of Suriname, man!"

He then described how, on their first date, she'd given him a blow job after smearing Nutella on his manhood.

"She sounds like a lovely girl…" Bill said, without a hint of a smirk.

We all bit our lips, as it went straight over Mick's head.

When Katy did arrive, we saw that she was easy on the eye and very intelligent. It was hard to put them together, because Mick was neither – but as the night went on, 'a bit of rough' came into the conversation. The sister, Sophie, also seemed to fancy a bit of rough and had taken a shine to me. She was a little dumpy, so I tried to point her Bill's way. Maybe he fancied a bit of Nutella. It was getting late now, and with the doubts still whirling around in my head, I needed to get out of there.

"I think I'll be off, now," I said, standing up and stretching. "I'm shagged. I need to get some sleep."

Seeing this, Al said, "Me too, mate. I'll go with you." Something in his eyes told me he felt the same as I did.

We made, arrangements to all meet up again, then me and Al left. We walked towards Putney, to try and catch a cab and as we talked, it all came out. He was in exactly the same boat as me – he just couldn't get his head round it, either.

It was getting late, but this needed to be talked through. And I knew exactly where we could go. I was very friendly with the landlady of a pub called the Star and Garter, on the river, in Putney. Jan would always give me a lock-back and even let me kip there, if I needed to. So that's where we sat, till about four in the morning, trying to make sense of it all.

Again, it went around in my head, and I had no faith in continuing with this venture. But then Al told me honestly why, even with his doubts, he wanted to go.

As I said before, Al hadn't joined 40 till after we'd come back from the Falklands War – and apart from NI, there was very little chance of any action at that time. He did four years, then sacked it out of boredom and before he ended up on a basket weaver's (Alcohol Awareness) course.

"This," he told me, "is a chance to see if I actually have the mettle."

His honesty was the thing that drew me to Al, and a bond was made. There might be some big timers out there, thinking 'this sounds a bit soft', but I'll tell you now – Alan Boydell went on to endure more fire fights than anybody else I have ever met or in any Special Forces memoirs I have ever read.

We left it there. Jan got him a taxi home and sorted me a bed upstairs; then she came to tuck me in. Pub landladies – you've got to love them.

The following day, we all briefly met up with John, and he told us he was returning home to the Isle of Wight, and would be coming back to London towards the end of the month. On that same date, he would be flying from London to Amsterdam, with Pat. John was now on very friendly terms with him and had stayed at his flat prior.

Suriname was a former Dutch colony – and because of the volatile situation, many of the Surinamese people had fled to the Netherlands for safety or economic reasons. It was these exiles who were willing to pay the most to get rid of Bouterse. John was now going to tell them he had his team together, and to make final arrangements for our move.

So – as easy as that, John would be taking his team of Pat, Mick, Bill, Al and – at that moment, at least – me, on a military operation in South America.

As you read this, (especially the soldiers) you are probably thinking *No fucking way. This is bollocks!* Well, I thought exactly the same thing.

However, to make sure I was up to speed for the task in hand, If, it ever arose, I spent most of my time fitness-training as I always did and reading up as much as I could about Suriname in the local library. Equipment and clothing wise I, was pretty good – there were just a couple of specific jungle items I needed, but I could easily get them from Army Surplus stores. There was one just down the road from my place in Streatham, so off I went.

The place had everything I needed, but just as I had paid for the items and was on my way out, something else caught my eye.

As I walked back in the sunshine, it seemed now, that even with all my doubts, I was wrapped up in it. My path to another future had stalled, so I now pictured myself going, after all. I would just have to wait and see if it was actually going to happen.

The end of August arrived and John and Pat flew to Schiphol. They were met by JC sympathisers and driven to Den Hague to meet the backers. They were away for four days, and very little info flowed back.

When they returned, we all met at Pat's flat, where he dished out envelopes filled with Dutch guilders that roughly worked out as £1000 each. This seemed to seal the deal, and everybody perked up considerably.

John then told us more of the plan and how we were getting there. "You'll fly from London Heathrow to Paris, where you'll meet a guy called Rajin. He's a refugee from Suriname and he's worked with me before – in '86," John said. "He's responsible for authorising your money transfers. From Paris, you'll fly to Cayenne, in French Guiana, via Martinique. Afterwards, you'll travel by road to the border town of St Laurent and from there, take a canoe across the Marowijne river to south of Albina, in Suriname."

We nodded as he went on. It all still sounded unbelievable to me, but here we were – looking committed. My suspicions were not alleviated by the way John was briefing us, though.

He tried to explain how we would get across the country, listing the villages that were pro or against the ruling government of Suriname, and what could be found in the various areas.

Now, this is all standard, as briefings before an Operation go, but he was doing this without any form of visuals – not even a map. Everyone – even Pat 'Mitty' – was thrown, but I think the fact we now had £1000 in our pockets kept us all quiet. This was the way it was to be with John: he seemed to have no idea. Not even at your basic Infantry Corporal level. I was beginning to question that he had been in the Legion for three weeks, never mind three years.

Everyone bit their tongue for the rest of the session, shook hands at the end and – hanging on to the money – departed. Now, again, we just had to wait.

Less than a week later, John announced that he was yet again going back to Holland – with any one member of the team – to make further arrangements. Everyone on the team agreed that it should be 'no-bull' Al – except Mick, who said his girlfriend didn't like Al (like I said, BONE!).

John wanted to drive there this time, so they left the next afternoon in John's grey Ford Sierra and took the ferry. They drove to the bar where John and Pat had stayed during their last visit, because John had struck up a relationship with the Bush Negro owner of the bar – Henna.

Now, I have said 'negro' earlier in this account, so before the PC brigade have a go – I will explain. Black slaves were taken from Africa by the Dutch to work in the harsh environment of South America. 'Bush Negro' or later, 'Maroon', is a term for the slaves who either escaped and lived by their wits or were given their freedom and a small piece of shitty jungle to survive in. Now away from the whip of the Dutch, they were very proud of this label, and at that time, that is who they would tell you they were.

Henna spoke to the barman and told him to get drinks for John and Al. Then, an argument ensued in Dutch. It was clear that the barman wasn't happy about the Englishmen drinking free beer all the time, but she replied by telling him to shut up – as it was her bar.

They stayed there for a couple of days, during which time John would frequently disappear on his own and come back to meet Al in the evenings. Then, something totally off the wall happened that could have ended the whole job.

Again, much to Al's annoyance, John had gone out in the morning alone, leaving Al watching MTV by himself in the flat above Henna's bar.

After hearing a series of creaks coming from the stairs, Al went to investigate. As he did so, he heard the sound of glass breaking in the lounge. But the footsteps now running up the stairs caught his full attention, and he spun round, his hands up ready for a fight.

Suddenly, a Heckler & Koch MP5 9 mm sub machine gun was pressed to his face and he was kicked in the stomach, propelling him backwards into the lounge. There, the patio doors had been smashed open and the lounge was now occupied by two more figures dressed in paramilitary uniforms with stun grenades and pointing machine guns at Al's head. He was held down and handcuffed, hearing Henna's screams of protest from the kitchen, as she too was handcuffed.

"What the fuck's going on?" Al demanded, but he was given no reply, except for a kick in the ribs and a hood placed over his head.

Al explained to me later that the whole assault took just a few seconds. He was then marched to the stairs, kicked down and thrown head first into a car, which sped off. He was then raced across the city and shoved into a very secure police cell.

Prior to this incident, John had also been arrested by two policemen in civilian clothing, who had calmly walked up to his car while he was in the driver's seat, jabbed a pistol into his face and dragged him out, onto the ground.

The unit that had arrested Al and John turned out to be the Dutch Anti-Terrorist Police, who were acting on a tip-off. After his initial anger at being taken, later on, Al only spoke of his admiration at the professionalism of these men. However, at the time, while still hooded and handcuffed, he wasn't so impressed, and loudly protested his treatment.

After Al had been left in his cell for an hour or so, shouting through the hood, the door opened and two or three men entered and proceeded to kick him viciously, telling him to 'shut the fuck up!' in their Dutch accents and calling him an 'Irish bastard'.

Although Al was English, and explained this, telling them to check his passport – his assailants were convinced that he was IRA and didn't believe that his name or his passport were real. After numerous failed attempts to explain that this was simply a case of mistaken identity, and still restrained by the handcuffs and blindfolded by the hood, Al told them to 'Get fucked!' and refused to cooperate.

After being left for another hour or so, another officer came in, removed Al's hood and handcuffs and admitted that a mistake had been made.

"I'm sorry, but we were given information that two men with Irish accents were staying in Henna's flat," he explained to Al. "We were told they had arrived in a grey Ford Sierra, carrying bags full of weapons."

Still unhappy, Al grudgingly accepted that it sounded like them, and acknowledged that they were only doing their job.

"Ah, and we know who your friend is, now – John Richards," the police officer said, with a wry smile. "He's quite famous around here, for his time in Suriname."

Al thought, *Bollocks! That's it, the job's all over.*

But the cop just winked and said, "Good luck!" as he set him free.

When John and Al got back to Henna's bar, the barman was nowhere to be seen. He'd done a runner. They recognised, then, that he was the one who had purposefully dropped them in the shit.

Although Al and John were both relieved that they hadn't been kidnapped and chopped up by Bouterse contacts in Holland, it had shaken them up and they now thought it was way too dangerous to stay. John said his goodbyes to Henna, and he and Al went back to England. John, yet again, went back to the Isle of Wight.

Al, after explaining to a gob-smacked audience what had happened, complained to us that John had consistently gone off on his own.

"Never once explained where he'd been," Al said, frowning. "Or who he'd been with."

"Same thing happened when I travelled with him," Pat agreed.

The air was tense. We weren't getting the whole story.

Chapter 3

Moving Out

John had called us all from the Isle of Wight. "The job's on," he said.

I have to admit, I felt a little surge of adrenalin. "Yeah?"

"Yup. I'll come over in the week and pick up Mick, seeing's as he speaks a bit of French. We'll head for Paris before you lot, to sort out the tickets and any last-minute details."

This now began to feel real. I quickly did my final admin, getting my last inoculations, malaria tablets and bought anything else I thought I might need. I also needed to clear up some personal matters and clarify that I was still on the right path. That was easier than I thought it would be, and now, other than my doubts about a couple of the people I was going with, I was committed.

True to his word, John came back that week, gave us all one hundred pounds each to get a plane ticket, and told us to meet in central Paris in two days' time. He and Mick then disappeared in John's car.

We did that and agreed to meet at an allotted time at Heathrow, deciding that it was best not to travel together in a group, so as not to draw attention to ourselves. This was ironic, because when we got to Heathrow I realised that we all looked like we were going off on safari (apart from Pat), so we stuck out like a sore thumb at the departure gate with all the suited business travellers on the BA flight to Charles De Gaulle.

When we got off in Paris, still pretending we didn't know each other, we went to the carousel to pick up our kit, and I got a bit of a shock.

I had all my military kit stuffed into a massive Bergan (rucksack) that I had tried to disguise a little with one of those big luminous covers. Al had his Bergan with no cover, but he was wearing one of those fishing jackets, so it made sense that people would think he was just going on a fishing trip.

Bill had one of those tiny little French A-frame backpacks you can barely fit a flask and some sandwiches in, looking like he was off on a painting holiday.

But Pat? Pat only had a small green, sports hold all and was dressed as if he was just going away for a dirty weekend! Although I was surprised, seeing him at check inn. I had imagined that he must have sent some kit over already, for him to pick up in Paris, but it turned out that he hadn't! I looked at the state of him and thought, *He really doesn't know what's going on here!* As entertaining as he was, I wasn't carrying him. Judging by the reactions of the others, neither were they.

We met up with John and Mick in central Paris and spent the night in a rundown hotel just off the Champs-Élysées. Mick took us to a couple of his old Legionnaire drinking dens, where Bill continued to showcased his fluency in French, while John did his usual disappearing act. It was now beginning to feel all very 'secret agent', what with a rendezvous in a seedy Paris bar and hushed talk in the corner, of overthrowing governments. Looking back, it all seemed very glamorous; however, even though I was only twenty-four years old, I had been through a lot and had a very old head on those young shoulders. As much as I was now slipping into the role – as we all did on the *Canberra* on our way south to the Falklands – I knew that things were not going to be so 'James Bond' when we got there.

We kept out of trouble and the next day, we went back to Charles De Gaulle where Rajin stood outside the terminal, waiting to meet us and see us off. He handed us our flight tickets, shook our hands vigorously and thanked us all very much for what we were about to do. As I looked at this casual smart man of Indian descent, I thought, *You're welcome mate. Just as long as I get my money.*

We all hovered around, while John then took him to one side and had a lengthy chat. When he had finished, he handed Rajin a sheet of paper. This, John told us later, was all our bank details – which we had given him previously – so Rajin could transfer all our monies. We then, decided to all split up again, as we had done in Heathrow, although Rajin had already taken this into account and none of our seats had been booked together.

We then continued through customs with the normal throng of passengers, who we now could blend in a little more with, and boarded the plane to Martinique without any trouble.

Sitting on my own, on the 747 for around eight hours gave me a lot of time for thought.

So, this is probably a good time to tell you, who I am.

I joined the Royal Marines as a spotty teenager of 16 in September 1980. In early 1981, I passed out of CTC (Commando Training Centre), with 270 Troop. By 1982, at eighteen, I was fighting the Argies in the Falklands War as one of the youngest members of the task force. At just turned nineteen in January 1983, I did my first tour of Northern Ireland in what was then the Badlands of South Armah, and in early 1984, at twenty, I had just passed Recce Troop Selection (elite training course) at 40 Commando, Royal Marines.

I was waiting for my parachute jump course – since all Recce Troop are jump-trained – and was enjoying going out 'on the pop', with a few old sweats from HQ Company. Unfortunately, me and a few others from HQ got into a huge fight. We had beaten up some civvies and smashed up a pub in Taunton: I think it was called The Half Moon. For very good reason, I might add. However, this proved to be a bit of a nail in my coffin, since I had been becoming a bit wild and this wasn't the only incident I had been embroiled in.

The police got involved and the OC (Officer Commanding) gave me and a mate of mine Mick Bowen, two weeks in camp jail and pulled me off my jumps course. Being the full-of-myself person that I was back then, after I got out of camp clink, I decided to put in my request to leave, thinking it might be better to pre-empt it, in case I was pushed. I already had my eyes on the SAS, so I thought this was as good a time as any.

After the sad goodbyes and proffing (stealing) as much of my military kit as I could, I moved down to Southampton with my lady friend. But when I went to the Army Careers office, I got a bit of a kick in the balls. To keep this short, the arseholes in the recruiting office – without a gong (combat medal) between them – said I would have to join a regular army unit, complete all the basic training, and *then* I could request SAS selection!

Bollocks to that! I thought, *so I moved back home north and had a try at the office there.* Again, same story. *Bollocks!*

But I had nowhere else to go, so I took it on the chin and went through the process. Now, with me being former Navy, you would think this would be simple. No. At the time, this actually made it more difficult. It would be months before I would even get to the Army selection centre.

Down in the dumps, I started hitting the drink and getting into a bit of shit. This wasn't good and I needed to get out of this downward spiral. Then, I saw an advert in the paper that said: 'Part-time Paratroopers Wanted'. Reading further, it was a TA centre in Norton, just near where I lived. *That's it!* I thought, *while I'm waiting, I'll join the part-time Paras.* A guaranteed, jumps course!

That Tuesday was what they call 'Drill Night', so I went along and they signed me up. The very next week, I was on P Company (Paratrooper Selection), down in Aldershot. And straight after that, I was at Brize Norton for my jumps course! It was as simple as that. Well, for those who have done it, maybe not so simple.

Anyway, at still just 21, I was now a Commando trained Paratrooper in D Coy 4 Para, or 'Dirty Delta' as they were known. I did still have my eye on the SAS, but things were taking forever at the regular recruiting office. They said I could have a place with the Royal Engineers in six months' time or, for Parachute Regiment, I would have to wait a year!

I have to admit, I was really enjoying 4 Para. The lads in D Coy were awesome and having the flexibility to go and soldier as and when you pleased, rather than *having* to, seemed to make you want to soldier better.

I had to make, a decision, but as life goes, it was actually made for me. The lads in Dirty D had been telling me about the SAS Reserve, up in a place called Prudhoe, about an hour from my home. They knew a few lads who had gone there, passed selection, and then gone on to pass regular selection at Hereford. Apart from the fact that I couldn't believe there was an actual SAS Reserve, that was now my path.

To make sure I was absolutely ready, for the whole of the next year, I went on every possible instructor course I could and trained like a madman.

At still only twenty-three when I began selection, I had already made full Corporal and was the fittest I had ever been. I was also very lucky, because a friend of mine, Barry O'Sullivan, who incidentally married one of Micks sisters, was already in, and I was constantly on the hills, training with him.

Now, blowing my own trumpet here, when I got to selection, I absolutely smashed it. So much so, that the DS thought I was cheating and on the individual tests, they took turns keeping tabs on me.

So, now you're thinking, *what the hell is he doing on that plane, with this lot?* But, as happens in life, things don't always go exactly as planned, and my security clearance had been flagged, so I couldn't go onto what they call 'continuation training'.

D Coy were not called Dirty Delta for nothing. They were the biggest, hardest – putting it nicely – pirates you could ever meet. At that time, even in the regular Parachute Battalions, they were notorious as people not to fuck with. I loved them and slipped very easily into their world – not completely, but I always knew what was going on. This, I thought, could have been another nail in the coffin, because Barry, who was also ex-D, had been flagged up with me. Barry had been in 23 SAS for almost two years and was already prepping for Hereford.

But since nothing had ever been proven, it turned out that operating on the edge of the law was not what had put us both on hold. We found out later from the head DS (directing staff) of 23 SAS, a good friend of Barry's, that it had been one of D Company's, officers, who had put the spanner in the works; although he'd had no evidence that we had done anything wrong, and rather than just confront us like a man, he stabbed us both in the back, telling the SAS that we both had been involved in some villainous activity.

Now the lads who have been vetted will know, that some villainous activity does not necessarily stop your SC (Security Clearance) or the higher DV (Developed Vetting). Given the levels of violence some of them have been involved in. Soldiers out there, would wonder how some of the animals (who I worked with later on in life) at SFSG (Special Forces Support Group), get theirs.

SC is not like that, I cannot go into the details, but a personal discrediting letter from your last OC will scupper it.

So, here I was, at the age of 24, sitting looking out the window of the plane. Still on hold, as the DS of 23 SAS, who saw the potential in both of us, were struggling to fight our corner with the CO (Commanding Officer). I knew they would make me do the last few hills again (seriously hard physical tests), but that just made me want to smash it even more, so I could rub that cock's face in it.

Many, many, years later, I met the man who had stabbed me in the back again at an old Airborne/SF reunion and charity event. He had no idea that I knew what he had done, and I couldn't help staring into his eyes and grinning like a Cheshire cat as I shook his hand. By then, he knew that rather than fucking me, his actions had actually sent me down a path even beyond this story – and by then, I had done way, way, more than I could have ever have done in the TA SAS.

So, that's who I am. But again, I am hearing you say, *If he wanted to continue with the SAS so much, why is he on that plane? There's no way he would get his security clearance, doing this sort of thing!*

Well, as I said before, things don't always go the way you think they will. And even before I'd put the thousand pounds in my pocket, another path had appeared from nowhere.

Touching down in Martinique, John told me that he, Mick and Pat would remain there for a couple of days, while the rest of us would travel onto Cayenne. This was news to us, but if it made us less conspicuous – no problem. We three then flew directly on to Cayenne.

As with Heathrow and Paris, customs here had just let us through without any problem. John had told us, "They'll just think you're Legionnaires based in Kourou."

I knew different.

On arrival, we booked into a small hotel run by JC sympathisers on the outskirts of the town. We then laid low, waiting for John and the others. "Just keep low-key," he had said.

Okay, pal, I thought, *I'll play the game.* Although John didn't seem to practice what he preached – because two days later, he arrived in Cayenne with a two-man French TV film crew! Al, Bill, and I couldn't believe it, but there was nothing we could do. John stated that this was his operation, to do with as he wanted, and we would just have to wear it.

The TV crew was the same one that had covered John in 1986/7, and he was clearly enjoying the notoriety. Despite Al and Bill's feelings of doubt, the crew were already here, so we were stuck with it.

Another person had also turned up with the team and TV crew: Ped. Al and I first laid eyes on him from the viewing gallery above the terminal, as he exited the plane.

"Who or what the fuck is that with Mick?" Al had asked.

Ped was Scandinavian, which was pretty obvious, because he was almost a cartoon caricature – he was heavily accented, with white/blond hair, and he had turned up at the airport dressed like a 70s porn star, in a white denim suit, steel-tipped cowboy boots and a red cravat. He had served with Mick in the 2nd Rep. He was a young, good-looking, likeable guy, and unlike Mick, he was bright. The more I got to know him, the more I liked him. With Ped, you got exactly what it said on the tin.

Although we were shocked – since nobody had told us that there would be another team member up to this point – for me, the more men we had like Ped, the better.

When they all first arrived, though, out of the blue – especially the film crew, I really *was* wrangling with the question of what I was doing here – and I was ready to get the next plane home. None of the others knew my situation completely – not even Al. But there were other pressures on me now; so again, I bit the bullet and kept my mouth shut.

Thankfully, the crew – Eric and Bernard – were amicable and agreed to blank the faces of anyone who didn't want to be seen. Also, they provided a pretext for us being there – we could now travel across the 200+ kilometres of French Guyana under the guise of being a film crew.

With all of us now in that shitty little hotel in Cayenne, John – again, without any map – laid out what we would do next. The TV crew would sort the transport; but there seemed to be no mention of any weapons for the crossing into Suriname. All of us were very concerned about this and after our complaining, John agreed to get some.

This, he did by simply buying them over the counter in a local gun store. Again, this was not my idea of laying low, but it was very easy to do in that country, back in those days. These were various types of pump action and double-barrelled shotguns – not what we wanted, but they would serve as some protection at least, until we got some automatic rifles from the JC.

The next morning, with the weapons strapped in some tarp under the minibus, we set off for St Laurent. There was no aircon in those days, except in very expensive cars, so we had all the windows open to let the air rush in. It was still hot, although the draught of air gave the illusion of cooling us.

Even with all my doubts, I knew, now, that I would be seeing this out to some sort of conclusion. So, as we continued down the road, warm air flowing through the van, I let myself enjoy that feeling you have with a group of soldiers off to do something that the guys in the army recruiting office could only dream about.

It felt strange, driving along the road – almost peaceful. Nobody really said very much, as if we were all absorbing what was around us. Going into some zone in which you emptied your mind of everything unnecessary, only concentrating on what you were about to do. The road was smooth, there were no checkpoints and we arrived into St Laurent, without a hitch before nightfall.

Again, we headed to a cheap hotel run by JC sympathisers. John immediately went to find the JC contact who would take us across the river to Suriname, but they never turned up. There was nothing we could do, so we spent the evening in the company of the film crew, all holed up in that small hotel. They were very interested in our backgrounds, which the Legionnaires seemed quite eager to tell – and Pat, especially, had some bullshit banter. I tried to keep my distance.

From the room that I now shared with Mick and Ped, you could see the river we would be crossing. With nothing to be done, we just sat drinking a beer, having a good crack and looking at the river. It all seemed very chilled, and with the windows open and the warm breeze flowing through, it was a pretty lazy way of getting acclimatised before we headed into the jungle. The weapons stayed on the bottom of the van and for security's sake, we had a watch organised throughout the night.

The next day, we stayed low in the rooms, while John went out to locate the guide again.

He came back cursing, but without giving us any information, other than the news that we would be moving out that night. Since we didn't know what he was cursing about, we were all reasonably confident that everything was on track, as we prepped to move from the hotel.

Now, though, the TV crew took this opportunity to pull out the cameras and start to interview everyone. As we were pulling the weapons from the vehicle, suiting up and laying on the cam cream, the camera was everywhere. I avoided it as best I could and pissed myself laughing at some of the things the boys were saying. But now the TV crew were pushing me.

"No! No," I said, shielding my face with one hand and holding the other one in front of the camera. "I told you, I don't want to be seen."

This was awkward. Mick and some of the others were looking at me, as if I thought I was something special. And I didn't want to cause any rifts already. So, after confirming again that they would disguise my face, I agreed.

Trying to keep it on track, I told them, "I'm a former weapons instructor and I'm here to teach, as a professional soldier…"

I thought I had covered my back a little, and that it came off okay. It will now probably be in some French news archive somewhere and I will no doubt, sound like a knob.

Then with that ordeal over, and us all ready to rock, we waited for the boatman.

While we waited, I looked around at the mix and match of uniforms and equipment in the room. For visual ID, we had all been asked to wear a green beret to identify us from the JC, who mainly wore red, and local soldiers, who mainly wore black. As for the rest of our kit, it all differed greatly.

Apart from his fishing jacket, me and Al looked pretty much the same. I had a set of camouflaged bottoms on from 23, a green T-shirt from No.1 PTS (Parachute Training school), a pair of standard lightweight high boots, my lightweight webbing from NI (Northern Ireland) and my old issue Bergan. I hadn't put my jungle shirt on, in case this seemed to be advertising a British invasion – and I was still trying to stay grey.

Mick and Ped, however, were in full Legion uniform and looked like poster children for the Legion recruiting office. Bearing in mind that we were now in a French colony, with a Legion barracks just up the road, I knew that this was a bad idea; but again, I kept shtum.

John was also in a green T-shirt, but he had green shorts on with his jungle boots and socks.

With his tiny backpack, he looked like a South African park ranger, or worse, something from the sit-com *It Ain't Half Hot Mum*. Bill looked pretty much the same – but I later realised that although they didn't look all Rambo, in the heat of where we were going, it was actually pretty effective clothing to wear.

Now, back to Pat – and things were not looking good. He had no military Bergan, some old 50s webbing from Army Surplus, a dark blue T-shirt, fashionable cargo pants and a pair of desert boots. If you'd taken the weapon from his hands, he'd have looked like part of the camera crew. Everyone in the team knew he was ballast – even John – but John just didn't seem to give a shit.

Then, looking out the window through the side of the curtains, John saw the boatman arrive. "He's here!"

He darted off, then a few minuet's later, called up to the room from the river below, "Move quickly! Out by the back stairs!" This exit led directly to the river.

With our weapons now in our hands and kitted out the way we were, this was a tense time and bumping into the local French plod could have ended up, very messy.

We sneaked down to the river, where two long, locally-made canoes with small outboards were waiting. After those of us with heavier kit had dropped it into the second boat, all seven of the team jumped into the first. As soon as we were in, the boatman pulled out and we waited just slightly offshore in the darkness, while the two men from the camera team loaded their equipment and themselves into the second boat. When they had pushed off, we all slipped away into the night.

The part of the river where we crossed was wide and the water was very fast-flowing. Luckily, the boatman seemed to know what he was doing, but that still didn't stop us all thinking that we could end up in the drink at any time. Trying to blot out thoughts of all the creatures with teeth in the water that could do you a real bad turn, I looked across towards the Suriname Army post at Albina, further north, on the other side of the river.

From the camp, I could see a searchlight dancing left and right, up and down the river. As we moved across with our weapons ready in the blackness, I couldn't help thinking that they knew we were coming.

Then, as the boat finally hit the bank on the other side, we leaped out, weapons ready, and automatically went into all round defence.

This was it. We were in.

Chapter 4

South of Albina

We remained there for some time, silent, listening to the noise of the bush and the water gently lapping against the bank of the river. I was now waiting for John to make the decision, to move out. It didn't happen.

I looked around at the others, who like me, looked a little uncomfortable, just waiting there. Even the camera team and the two boatmen were looking as if to say, what the hell was happening. SOPs (Standard Operating Procedures) would now be, to move away from the landing point asap, but as I looked across at John, he seemed oblivious.

I then eyed Mick and between us, we knew that this merry band, needed some proper leadership.

I let Mick make the first move and he turned to John and whispered that we should move out, John just said, "ye, okay," but made no movement to say he was going to do so.

Thankfully, I thought to myself, Mick may be bone, but at least his soldiering skills seem okay. Mick then turned to the boatman, Edward, who would also be our guide, and asked him to lead us somewhere safer, away from the water.

This he did in French, but Micks French, was basic Legion French and a lot of Frenchmen would struggle to understand it, as did Edward.

Mick, then began to get frustrated and louder, as he tried again and again to get the guide to understand.

This was now getting stupid and as I looked at the two, camera team, I felt almost embarrassed.

Then a calm quiet voice piped up, in fluent French, that the guide could understand and explained what had to be done. I turned to Bill, who had now gone back to looking toward the bush, ignoring what was going on behind him, crouched there just doing his job.

Over the years, I have been on some seriously difficult courses. As an instructor on some myself, you still do the same thing.

You scan the room to size everyone up, trying to gage who looks like they are going to pass and who is going to fail. What I have found, is that there is always a quiet one in the corner, who doesn't look much, but ends up really surprising you. As the job continued, Bill was that man.

As we quickly grabbed our Bergan's, Edward led us off, as the other boatman helped the camera team out of the boat.

As we moved through the bush to a track that skirted the riverbank, we were now all in full Op alert mode, weapons in the shoulder, eyes on the jungle. As we got to the track and continued along, this now started to look a bit odd, as our guide up front, was just strolling, along, in the middle of the track, with his hands in his pockets. I was a bit worried he was going to start whistling a tune. On seeing this, we didn't exactly switch off, but the tension came down a notch or two.

After about a k or so, a less prominent path went off to the left, which he took and after a few hundred metres we were looking at a small rundown shack in the bush. He then just walked straight to the front door and gestured us to do the same. Now fingers closer to triggers again and with a bemused guide looking on, we tactically occupied the building.

The place was in a bad way, no one had lived in there for quite some time and a large amount, of insects where scurrying about the place, including some big nasty looking spiders.

As we cleared some space and looked around for somewhere to doss (Sleep) for the night, I looked into what was the bedroom. There were two old iron single beds, with heavily stained mattresses on top, I had a look under one and saw a huge snake skin that had recently been shed. As I stood up, John and Mick where now looking in. "All yours, gents," I said, as I gave John a Mickey Mouse salute and went back into the other room with the rest of the team.

The camera team, with the other boatman then arrived, as we went into normal routine, of checking weapons, sorting out arcs of fire and feeding etc. Then as the other boatman went back to stay with the boats for now and a guard rotor sorted, we settled in.

Just as we did there was a loud cry from the bathroom, it was John and he burst out with his pants half way down his legs. "Jesus," he said, "someone go in there and kill that fucking spider." He looked at me, *soft git,* I thought and I stood up and made my way into the bathroom.

"Jesus!" I had never seen anything like it, it was as big as a dinner plate and with legs as thick as a hair brush. However,

I couldn't back out now, so I got the butt of my shotgun and hit it as hard as I could. 'fuck' the thing was solid, so again and again I hit it until it's insides spewed out. I don't want to sound like a pansy, but it made me feel a bit sick.

I bluffed it when I went back in the main room, with a manly swagger, but I did not sleep soundly that night.

As daylight broke, Edward was already getting on a brew. As he sat and boiled the water, I could now study his face more. He was young, in his late teens early 20s, he looked at me with a big grin on his face and seemed like he didn't have a care in the world. I tried to speak to him in English and realised he did understand a little, but replying was not so easy.

Bill then began a long conversation with him in French. At first it seemed all jovial, but then Bills mood changed a little and he looked and listened more intensely at the guide. John and Mick had now come out onto the porch and Bill glared over to John, something was wrong.

I couldn't understand the conversation, but as Bill looked at John, John looked as if he had been caught by the school teacher, doing something very naughty.

Bill stood up and said to John, "I think we should do a quick patrol round the immediate area." Then, without giving John time to answer, he picked up his weapon and asked me to go with him.

Seeing something was wrong, I grabbed my weapon and joined him. As we did a quick perimeter check, still within sight of the shack, I asked Bill what was wrong.

Without hesitation he explained. The boatman and guide, where not our JC contacts at all, John had just gone into town and asked around for anyone to take us across the river.

They were here, just because John had paid them.

My stomach sank a little as I thought about what could have happened. The guide could have taken a bribe and lead us all straight into the arms of the Suriname Army. For all we knew they could have been waiting in that shack, ready to mow us down, before we even got started.

As we continued with the patrol, the doubt in my stomach about John, was now just getting bigger and bigger.

As we got back, the team was outside having a brew and eating what they brought. John, then told everyone, we would be patrolling the area and keeping an eye out for army patrols, while we wait for someone from the JC to come and pick us up.

"This is also a good time," he said, "for the camera team to get some footage of us in the jungle."

"Come on, they will make you all famous." He was now pathetically trying to boost up the troops, as the day went on and the rest of the boys found out what we knew. He was wasting his time.

I did notice though, that as the day went on, Mick now already seemed to be trying to steal Johns thunder as leader.

He also seemed to be wanting more and more, the attention of the camera. Pat had also got very clubby and began helping them with their kit. I had the feeling, if he could, he would have put down his weapon and joined them.

In this very short period of time, the dynamics of the team seemed to be unfolding and as I quickly interpreted, not to the liking of the camera team.

I don't know whether it was the camera that was making Mick act like a cock, but deep down I had the hunch, he already was. Throughout the day, I could now see the camera boys beginning to think twice, about trudging through the jungle with us.

By late afternoon and back at the shack, still no one from the JC had turned up and the grumbling became louder.

John then came up with the idea, that two of us would pop into the water with a rope and drift down the river to the gunboat that was moored at the army camp in Albina and steal it.

I don't think he was serious, just trying to big himself up to the TV crew, but looking at them, it had the complete opposite effect.

However, if the JC didn't come soon, we would need some transport, to get to the JC's main base in Moengo. It was decided to chance, going toward Albina camp that night and looking for some, just in case.

Eric and Bernard, politely declined Johns offer to go with them and somehow, Pat, had wrangled himself as rear party to keep an eye, on our now HQ.

My stomach was now churning to the point of nausea, as to what was going on around me, but John ultimately, at this time, still held all the cards.

Again, I had to hold my feelings back and told myself to just concentrate, on trying to stay alive, following this fucking idiot.

We would split into two teams, me and Bill would do a CTR (Close Target Recce) of the army camp and keep eyes on any movement from there. The rest of the boys would skirt the village surrounding the camp and look for a 4x4 to take if needed.

As john began to spell out how we were to do this for the camera, again without a map, I got pissed off, pulled out the one I had and threw it at him.

The twat couldn't even orientate it, but at least the lads had some visuals.

That done we moved out as soon as it got dark and headed for Albina. As we got closer, me and Bill peeled off to dick (observe) the camp and as we left the others I began to have doubts that Bill might not be up to it.

Again, I needn't have worried, his skills where spot on and we very quickly adapted that flow of movement that doesn't need a word spoken.

We got to a good spot near the camp and settled ourselves in, we now had a few hours to kill before the others retuned.

This was a quick awakening to some of the conditions we would be coping with for the rest of the job. The area around the camp was very wet and marsh like and the mozzies were absolutely brutal and tortured us to death as we crouched in the long grass.

It is a difficult choice in a situation like this, we could of, put shit loads of repellent on, but it is pungent and the smell carries. So, as we did not know what level of soldiers, the Suriname Army where, we played it safe and kept the repellent to a minimum.

I don't think it was only the lack of repellent, it's something about when you're new to the environment. As your something fresh, it seems that everything wants to come and have a taste of you. That's just the way it is and you just have to suck it up, lesson learned.

As we looked on, the camp was lit up like a Christmas tree and it was easy from where we, where, to see all the comings and goings. As it was, there were no coming and goings and the place seemed as if it was on lockdown. This was good for us as the boys would be safer moving around the village, but it just confirmed to me more that they knew we were here.

When we met back up, at the time and point arranged, things didn't look good. They couldn't find anything suitable and the mood was sour as we entered the shack.

Knowing now that our guide wasn't who we thought he was, people didn't rest so easy that night. Being now unable to sleep again, I found myself very easily, shooting the shit all night with Eric and Bernard, not about soldiering, just life in general, they just seemed to be on the same wave length.

Very early that next morning, the alarm went up, Ped had noticed movement on the path toward us. We all grabbed our weapons, legged it out of the shack and laid wait in the bush along the track. Then we watched, as some old black guy shuffled in his flip flops, toward the building. Seeing there was no immediate threat, we slowly came out of the bush with our weapons down. The old man gave a sheepish smile and waved at us. Then the poor old bugger shit himself, as Mick had now grabbed him by his jacket and was shaking him violently.

He screamed at him in French, asking who he was with and were there any troops with him. The bloke just started crying, saying he didn't understand. This again was firing Mick up and the man now thought Mick was going to kill him.

All this happened as Eric and Bernard had come to see what was going on and I saw Eric snap a picture. That picture ended up in a French combat magazine and it still sickens me, to look at what Mick did that day, frightening the shit out of this old guy, trying to be the big man.

Bill again jumped in, separated them and tried to calm the old man down. Mick then just headed off shouting, "Nobody fucks with us man," with John and Ped following.

John was laughing saying, "Silly old cunt," it sounded real, awkward the way he said it, like he was now sucking up to Mick. Ped looked back at me and although Mick was his mate, he too was not happy, with what he had just witnessed.

We were all now fussing over the old man, giving him a drink and Bill asked him if he wanted some food, or a smoke. He did the sign for a cigarette and Al lit one, he could hardly get it to his mouth, he was shaking so much.

I then had to try and calm Al down, as he now wanted to go and kick Micks teeth in. Again, as you read this, especially all the soldiers out there, it's hard to comprehend how this can happen.

Being there, for me it was simple. First you had a team, with possibly the worst commander you could ever have, put that with a group, all from different units, who had never worked together. Then put them in a place with absolutely, no back up and give them pea shooters against machine guns.

Now the people who just whinge about it all, are the ones that would not make my list. The ones that make my list, are the ones who adapt and get on with the job of changing things.

That was now my remit and as the old man began to get himself back together, I became even more determined to see this through.

Then, as Edward gave the old man some money to keep quiet and helped him back on his way.

I looked at Pat just stood there, pale, white and looked like he was going to be sick.

Eric and Bernard looked the same and there and then, I knew all of them wanted no more of this.

They then went back to the shack and immediately started to pack away their kit. We waited where we were for the time being as I still thought if Al goes anywhere near Mick right now, there will be blood and teeth everywhere. It wasn't long before they came back and after a long chat with our guide, Eric approached me.

He told me what I already knew, but it was the way he said it, that threw me a little.

In the short space of time they were with us, you just couldn't help but like them both. They seemed very genuine and were both very passionate about what they did.

I actually enjoyed their company, more than some of my fellow soldiers.

Eric then put his hand on my arm and with great warmth, said I should go too, "This," he said in his French accent, "was not a good place for you." I understood completely what he was telling me and it saddened me to try and explain, that I had to stay.

There was a moment and then he nodded his understanding, as Bernard then came over and shook my hand warmly. Given all have said about not wanting them there and staying Grey, I realised I would actually miss them.

Then Pat approached, again I knew what was coming. I wasn't to bothered about Pat leaving, I thought he would just become a burden. Since we had been there, he hadn't made himself any hot food and had been living off chocolate. He didn't have any basic stuff that can keep you alive in this environment, water filter, puritabs, salt tabs, nothing. He had a big shiny knife, that he had taped to his old webbing, but he wouldn't have lasted a week, outside of a Travelodge.

Saying all that and looking at him them, I couldn't help but feel sorry for him, he looked pathetic.

He then said, he would be escorting the TV crew back and would then bring some more supplies back for us. Who did he think he was kidding, anyway, I shook his hand and went along with the lie, to try and give him back some dignity. Then me Al and Bill waved them off, as they quickly disappeared down the track with our guide.

Now as me Al and Bill stood there, watching them go and knowing that our chance of a ride out of there was slipping away, an understanding was made, to watch each other's backs.

When I got back many months later, I found I shouldn't have felt so sorry for Pat. As soon as he got home, he went straight to the papers with unbelievable stories of him in the jungle, helping the Rebels and saving the lives of a film crew, he just happened to have pictures of, him and the film crew, that he had taken, when we were off risking it near Albina.

I have met many Walters over the years, but Pat Baker, well, he gets the gold medal.

With Al calmed down a little, we now returned to the even more sour atmosphere of the shack, as a decision had to be made, fast. Our location was now well and truly blown and we needed to get out of there. We told them that the TV crew and Pat had gone and wouldn't be coming back, zero response.

John then said, we would have to go and meet the JC and get to Moengo on foot.

Now this was over 40 km away, across the jungle, trying to avoid army patrols, with armoured vehicles and heavy weapons, with the six of us, carrying only shotguns.

You can imagine how popular he was, as he finished saying it. But again, apart from legging it back to the boats before they left and without any money to show for it, John still held all the Aces.

So, we packed up our kit, filled our water bottles and waited a couple of k away from the shack, in the jungle. Then as the sun was beginning to set we headed off.

To walk the 40 km direct through the jungle would have taken us forever, so till it got completely dark we skirted the main road, but still keeping as close to the bush as we could. I say main road, it was more like a large tarmac path with a lot of holes in it. Then later as darkness fell, knowing we would see lights of vehicles approaching we ventured out onto better ground and picked up speed.

John said, not to worry to, much about the Army now, as they don't like to go out at night. Forgive me if I didn't entirely believe him, but it was, now so much easier out on tarmac.

We then walked pretty much non, stop through the night, to get as much distance as we could from Albina.

I was on my game with fitness at that time and the walk was nothing I hadn't done before, but bearing in mind we had very little time to acclimatise, the heat was bad. As I looked around at the rest, I was actually a little impressed, especially with Bill as even though he was struggling, he just kept pushing on.

Al was still smiling, even though I knew he was suffering with some serious blisters, brought on by his brand, new French jungle boots he had bought in Cayenne.

John was walking along, hunched over smoking and trying to cover the light by curling his hand around it.

Mick was striding out front, he had told us and the camera team earlier, that his nick name in the Legion had been, The Colonel. "Ye man, that's what they called me, Colonel Mick man." A role he now seemed to be taking to hart.

Then Ped, bounding along behind like some large boy scout, just grinning like fuck.

As we went through the night, listening to the monkeys and birds crying out, I tried to get some focus. Things had to change, but at that time I really couldn't think how I was going to make that change. I would now be watching Colonel Mick very closely, to see how he was going to play it, then for now, make my decision based on that.

It was a really strange place to find yourself, no real command structure, no specific orders and not really knowing that if the shit hit, who would hold the line next to you.

Those feelings where to stay with me, for some time.

As the sun broke and lit up the tree tops, it looked absolutely beautiful, but as it rose, the heat got worse and people now were beginning to feel it. The pace dropped right off and we still had a fair way to go. The road was also beginning to disappear down to a small track through the bush and most of it, was overgrown.

As the pace got slower, I also saw the discipline begin to go.

Mick began to drop back now and he asked john to take, point as it was getting more and more difficult to navigate and john should know the way.

Mick then closed in on me, with his face as red as a beetroot and anger coursing through his body, "The first chance I get," he whispered, gesturing to John, "I am gonna kill that fucking cunt." Already it seemed, this was all going completely tits up and it confirmed my reasons for keeping a sharp eye on Mick.

Knowing that in daylight we needed to get out of the open and it may take all day to get to Moengo. We got to the stage of thinking about holding up for a while out of the sun, to get some rest. Water was now an issue in this heat and we would have to look for some. John had told us we didn't need to bring any rations, as the JC would be feeding us. Thankfully we had all ignored him and brought enough for a few days, however that was now running short.

Then as I began to see the body language of people on the verge of jacking, we received a sharp wakeup call, in the form of three pick, up trucks headed right toward us.

We heard them before we saw them and dashed deep into the bush, with weapons at the ready.

The trucks all had two, heavily armed men in the back, who looked like they meant business, so with our feeble shotguns aimed at them, we stayed put. Then we saw John, suddenly, running out and waving them down. He had a quick conversation, with the guy in the lead truck and then shouted to us, to come out.

We then all carefully headed to the wagons and as we got there, the men all jumped out and started to shake our hands. We had just made contact, with the Jungle Commando.

They told us to jump in, then they spun the vehicles around and raced back the way they came. They gave us some food and water, but best of all, we could now relax a little, taking the rest of the journey in the back of the trucks with a bit more firepower.

As we sped towards our destination, we passed the village of Moengo Tapu, overgrown by trees and vines. We were told by the men, how all the people there, had been killed and the village burned. The first town I saw, being one of ruin and desolation, sobered me up, as to where I was going.

We reached Moengo just as the sun was setting and were taken to an athletic track where a guy was selling booze under the grandstand, which the JC called The Sports Bar.

Along with the rest of the town, it looked tired.

The town had been built by the Dutch years before and as with all these former colonies upon independence, had fallen into ruin.

As we entered, the 'bar', it was filled with heavily armed JC, but what seemed a good atmosphere. We were glad of a beer, some food and to relax, but as we didn't really know these people or the area yet, we stayed on guard, wary of what and how much we drank.

John was now chatting up a storm with everyone he knew and at this point it seemed as if the job wouldn't be so bad.

That changed within the next hour, when two JC started a loud argument in taki-taki (the local language which just means talk-talk). I then heard a gunshot and as I spun round with my finger on the trigger, one of the two men was now crouched on the floor, screaming and holding his stomach, while the other stood above him with a revolver in his hand.

We all went defensive, weapons at the ready, as some of the JC tried to calm us down, while others wrestled the gun out of the shooter's hands. When the two men had been taken away, John explained to us, that here in Moengo, this happened all the time.

We'd been on the move now for two days, with very little sleep and we were all hanging. We wanted to leave the now soured atmosphere and just lay down. So, we were then, driven to the centre of town and taken into a large YMCA building, the JC HQ.

After splitting up into two groups of three into the dorm like rooms, (I was with Al and Bill, and John went with Mick and Ped), it just seemed to happen naturally that way and that was the way it was to stay. As we settled in, we decided that despite us all wanting desperately to sleep, at least one of us should stay awake and a rotor was done.

As I lay on my bed that night, in the YMCA building, I could not help but question what the fuck I was doing here. As I thought about the guy who had just been shot and then with Johns remark and how this had happened, within only hours of us being here. It made me think about how little value, life seemed to have here.

Chapter 5
The JC

The next morning, the HQ was buzzing, as everyone was preparing for the arrival of Ronnie Brunsjwick, the leader of the JC. At first, we were wondering what was so special about him, but it was easy to see the moment we saw him.

(Ronnie, only a couple of years older than me, seemed like a stereotype of every African Coup leader you've ever seen. He was covered in shiny badges and wore a red beret on top of his dreadlocks, with French paratrooper wings as a cap badge, which is a BIG shiny badge. He was friendly, charismatic, and looked upon as a Robin Hood figure by the local population. You could see why people were so willing to follow him. I myself looking at him, with his big smiling face, couldn't help but warm to him).

With him, were two personal bodyguards and a heavily armed entourage, who all smelled of weed. He came and shook all our hands and then had a very friendly quick chat with John. Then he went into the dining room with a few of his entourage and some other people who had been waiting for him. As the doors shut behind them, It, all went very quiet and it all seemed a little awkward in the room, until boom, the doors bust open and in a whirl wind, he was gone.

One of the people he'd spoken to in the HQ was Joseph.

(Joseph, an Asian looking man, I'm guessing in his early 40s, though his face didn't show it. He was a very quiet, observant man, a diplomat, and very prominent figure in the JC. He was also to be very helpful to me in future events).

Next to Joseph was Castro.

(Castro was Ronnie's right-hand man and enforcer. In his early 30s, he was the opposite to Ronnie in the way that he dressed and his persona. His uniform was immaculate, and he never seemed to smile. I grew to dislike him and felt he was never someone to cross).

Seeing Ronnie's heavily armed bodyguards, had made our shotguns look pathetic in comparison. We had to get some real weapons soon, so I spoke to John on the subject. He didn't seem that bothered and looking at me like I was already causing him a problem said, "Things move slow out here, you will just have to wait."

That same day, we were told to get into some trucks and they took us to the main JC camp in the jungle, It, was only about 20 minutes away and as we forded the river it was built next to, not too impressive. It was basically one giant open sided long hut, with hammocks strewn out and a big cooking pot at one end, with a few tables and chairs around it.

Over the next week or so, the other three had been sent off somewhere so me Al and Bill stayed there, doing the most basic infantry training program of weapon training.

First, we did the basic weapon safety drills, then set up a range, as we thought they must have some sort of knowledge. But as we tried to get them to hit a target at 100 m, we realised we had to go right back to basics.

Nobody held the weapon correctly and no one could hit a thing. Some of the weapons wouldn't even fire and one even split apart when he pulled the trigger. This seemed to get all their backs right up, as we had now embarrassed them a little.

Not a good start, but the problem was a simple one. As we looked at the weapons more closely, they were absolutely gopping (filthy). We now just had to demonstrate the simple art of cleaning a rifle.

Most of the weapons they had, where Belgian FN Fals, automatic versions of the SLRs (self-loading rifles) that me and Al had used as part of our normal training.

We both had brought some SLR cleaning tools and some 4x2 (correct size cleaning cloth). There wasn't much rifle oil to go around, but as we began looking at some of the older models and to the amazement of the JC who didn't even know they were there. There were oil bottles and some cleaning tools built into the stocks of the weapons themselves.

This dark magic was now to our favour and when we finally got them cleaned, we began adjusting sights, bringing them on target and making a few friends.

Basic weapon training is boring, I know this, so to keep things lively, we would throw in a few physical sessions, that some joined in, and some didn't.

We tried to make the fitness sessions a bit of fun, by making it more of a competition.

Press ups, pull ups and sprints all the usual stuff, but a real basic way of pulling people together into a trained group.

Even though I couldn't continue with the more need to know, continuation training in 23. Previously I had been sent on the first of many, Jap Slapping (unarmed combat) courses I did over the years, run by the SAS and the Royal Marines. It was absolutely nail's and I had come back quite sharp.

So, the real knives came out and I showed them a few moves, they loved it.

As the training continued we really began to like it at the camp, even with the shit food. Then something, that made me quite emotional happened. A truck had arrived with the usual supplies and the JC called us over to look at something.

In the back were three FN Fals in very good condition, with magazines and an ammo box full of lose 762 rounds (ammunition). I thought fuck you John, as Omleo, the head of the camp told us they were ours.

A couple of years prior with the Paras, I had gone on the first of many, of those exchange trips to the US. It was hosted by the US Rangers, who I thought were pretty good.

They also had with them a couple of Green Berets, who were instructing on some of the more exotic weaponry and also running the parachute jump program we were doing from Chinooks and Huey's.

Now these guys, were some of the coolest guys I have ever met, they all knew their stuff, but it was the matter-of-fact way they did it, that impressed me.

No bullshit and they were genuinely interested in where you come from and what you did.

During the Vietnam war they had proved invaluable at setting up training camps, field hospitals and generally being useful to the locals. They trained in dentistry, surgery and things that the population needed, other than just another grunt.

Today if the US wanted some dictator taken out, you would probably say, Navy Seals. If you wanted to influence the population and win a war, I would say, Green Berets.

Still in my opinion one of the best Special Forces units in the US.

At the end of the Falklands war, we had flown over from east island by helicopter, to take the surrender of west island. Once the head shed had done there thing, we had been tasked to escort the Argies back to the ships that would take them home. As they came down from the hills, cold, tired, wet and hungry, we were all on edge as they outnumbered us hundreds to one and it felt like it could end badly, very quickly.

Then some of the lads began handing out some of their Ration Packs to the starving soldiers, going past. That simple act, seemed to diffuse the situation in an instant and I never forgot it.

It was now in this camp, with Al as main armorer/weapons instructor and Bill fast becoming known as the professor, for his knowledge of all sorts of shit. Including setting up a water filtration system from the slightly murky river that flowed through. I took the role of senior DS and continued to try and build it all, into an organised unit, with a rank structure and with the help of Omleo, some sort of discipline.

In just a couple of days, the Green Beret angle, seemed to be working.

Over the time we spent in the camp, we had not seen the other three at all and we were beginning to wonder what was happening. The men in the camp that came and went at regular intervals, said that the others had been sent onto a VCP in another part of the JC controlled area.

Feeling a bit out of the loop and thinking for now, we had done enough basic in the camp itself, I asked if we could be more help back in Moengo and elsewhere. They said they would ask and Castro came the next day and took us back to Moengo.

We met back up with the rest of the boys and it all seemed very pally again. They told us what they had been doing and it sounded like they were having a right old time. I was a little bit jealous at first, but was glad things were now beginning to go a bit more smoothly.

I did see a few feathers were ruffling at the sight of our new weapons, but I thought it won't be long before they get some and all will be well.

With the YMCA as our new base, we were then tasked, like the rest of the team with going on patrol with members of the JC and to get to know the local areas. We would now be doing this on a rotor, so we could be in two places at once and cover more ground. Again, going all Green Beret, me Al and Bill were very friendly with the civpop (civilian population) and as we patrolled, we gently persuaded the JC to patrol properly. Spacing them out, showing some basic hand signals and what to do if someone started firing at us.

As we patrolled back into town and with the JC looking all very professional, the locals would come out and watch us. With this new approach, the kids then began to copy the actions of the JC.

They all had a bit of your, mans, man attitude and I thought they might get a bit pissed off with the kids. I couldn't have been more wrong and they lapped it up. After that we had no end of people wanting to patrol with us around town.

I have been bashing Mick in the story so far, but other than his map reading, (which he had absolutely no clue) his other soldiering skills seemed fine. He looked the part as did Ped and they seemed to make a good team. We had a good laugh when we were in the local bar and I really liked Ped's easy, going attitude. However, I could not warm to John, my gut was still saying he was a wrong un and my gut is always right.

Then as the days moved into weeks, Ronnie began moving us around to various points, much further afield and not quite under his control, into what was deemed enemy territory. It was simple to understand what he was doing, he wanted Bouterse to see, he now had a new big stick. Already it seemed, the parameters were moving and as things seemed to be going so smoothly, I was all too willing to move along with them.

This was how it was to be for the next few weeks, moving from place to place and keeping a presence within the community. It felt like a friendly, hot and sunny NI tour. We worked hard, but every now and then, we would all be in Moengo together, enjoying a bit of R and R, and having a few beers.

That said, the feathers were still ruffled about our better weapons and I began to see tiny cracks in the dynamics of the two teams.

Also, I saw that the weapon thing wasn't the only thing, that was beginning to divide us.

John was not the leader type, so Mick was more and more trying to become the voice of authority. This wasn't working with me Al and Bill, which I could see was winding him up.

This was then compounded by the way the JC acted toward us and them, quite frankly they thought he was a bit simple.

I had always thought that you don't command respect, you earn it. So, me Al and Bill continued to try and do just that.

We went out of our way to try and help in the local community and build up a rapport. As things progressed through our time there, this attitude I thought, was to help keep us alive. Now the selfish bit, it also helped us ingratiate ourselves with some of the local ladies, so everyone's a winner.

Me Al and Bill now began to work really good as a team, everyone had a different way they did things, but It all seemed just to, gel together really well. As we moved around the jungle, getting more Ferrell by the day, a strong friendship was built up and each day, without Johns presence, we just felt better and better about being there.

At that time, the rose, coloured glasses were firmly on and we went full bore into the role of training freedom fighters.

What was really good though, was that the locals began to confide that they were not so happy with John and his team. When they did bother to go to some of the outlying villages, there sense of superiority, was really getting on the local's nerves.

With this as a little boost, our group continued to get a little braver and we began, first out of curiosity, but later to see if we could complete the task first given, to move out further and further west within the country.

There was a particular place our little gang liked to go, upriver toward Tamarin, that had a large American missionary compound. We had now acquired a boat, by being overly nice to the local mine manager, to use for fishing and travelling to villages that were on the banks of the river. If we were going that way, we always asked Hass the local police chief if he wanted to come along.

(Hass the local police chief was a Hindustani in his late 20s. He'd had a hard time keeping law and order throughout the conflict and was keen to show us the areas he worked in. I figured it was beneficial to have our fire power with him and he was the one who had introduced us to the missionaries).

Actually, the first time we met the missionaries, it had gone a bit wobbly.

We were plodding along the river, with Al steering the outboard at the back and Madman as shotgun up front

(Madman was an exiled Cuban in his early 30s. His real name was Madane, but we nicknamed him Madman, as he was the craziest bastard there. He was a good soldier though, volunteering for training demonstrations and always wanting to go on patrol with us. He followed us around everywhere, and became the unofficial fourth member of our team).

With me Bill and Hass chatting and enjoying the ride, Al then threw the boat over to the right violently, nearly losing the engine off the back and the rest of us out the side. As Madman raised his weapon and Al shouted, "Enemy boat," we slammed into the bank, jumped out and got ready for a firefight.

Before we began shooting, we had to confirm who was in the other boat and we couldn't quite see yet. Hass then jumped up and began waving at the people in the other boat.

Crouched now behind our tiny boat, we then stood up to act more macho, as we looked at the large gleaming, very expensive speed boat, that was now approaching.

Then the chests went out further, as we saw the passenger was blond, very pretty and wearing a nurse's uniform.

The driver was the head of the church they belonged too, tanned and with his grey hair swept back, he looked very suave. We in contrast, with our sweaty combat clothing and cam cream, looked like a right bunch of tramps.

Hass then introduced us and acting like they had seen it all before, they asked if we would like a tow to their facility. Looking at nursey, we all said we would love to, so off we went.

They showed us the work they did here, the small medical facility they had and we had a really good time with everyone at the camp. Unfortunately, nursey was already married, to god, so no chance there, but we went back many times, as they were just, such nice people and the cookies and lemonade 'yes really' were spot on.

Even though we had seemed to win over the villagers, the local teachers (all ladies), in the main school of Moengo would ignore us and move the children along if they saw us.

This was bothering me a little now, so, one day patrolling the town and passing the local open-air pool where the school kids were having lessons, we went in to have a look.

All the children, along with the teachers, stopped what they were doing and just stared at us.

Right that's it, I thought. So, I put down my weapon, took off my uniform to a pair of shorts beneath, climbed the high diving board and did a back somersault into the pool below.

That seemed to break the ice, the kids all cheered and surrounded us and I got a round of applause from the teachers.

After that, the school children would constantly wave and run up to us in the street and while the teachers would initially hurry them along, they too after a after a while, started waving. Like I said, every one's a winner.

We continued training the JC as and when we could. They asked us about making bombs and as they had very little in the way of grenades or mortars, we went about trying to help. I had done a, couple of courses with the Royal Engineers that gave me some limited knowledge, but Bill was off the scale with his. We needed explosive material to start with, so the JC took us to the local Bauxite Mine, where we had acquired the boat.

It was there we found out just how far Ronnie's influence went, as we were able to go straight through security, into rooms filled with enormous amounts of various explosives. Of which we could take whatever we wanted, only having to sign for it, (you can imagine the range of Disney signatures and Winston Churchill seemed to love PE).

We even took a double cab truck, to carry it all in and use as a QRF (Quick Reaction Force) vehicle and since it was bright white, we spent an afternoon painting it camouflage with spray cans.

The JC wanted to help; they thought it was hilarious. A mine worker even welded a heavy machine gun bracket on the top, while Al whistled the A-Team tune. The whole situation was surreal.

Bill then got on really well with the mines, Dutch main demolition engineer and I know he wasn't supposed to, but he began helping us build up a river defence network. You could get from Paramaribo to Moengo by the river and this was bothering Castro. So, with Bill and the Dutchman supervising, me and Al began to lay a load of dem's that could be set with a single large car battery, if a couple of Bouterse's gunboats came steaming in.

We let Castro see and hear a couple of very loud demos and he was over the, moon, the only trouble was, he was very worried about any of the JC being responsible for letting it off. So, after a little money passed hands, the mine security guards, who seemed a little more responsible, agreed to secretly take on the task. That was the way it was here, everyone had a price.

Looking back now as I begin write this at the age of 55, I would love to live it all again. Really, we were just a group of kids, but we were making, a very serious impact.

However, as I looked deeper at what was going on around me, slowly things were beginning to change and my rose, coloured glasses began to slide off a little.

One night we were at a VCP, with Al and Madman at the barrier. Earlier in the day we had lifted and shifted a load of trees out onto the road with the JC, showing them how to slow the cars down as they approached. I was now laid in my hammock next to Bill in his, trying, but failing to get to sleep with mosquitos furiously biting.

Then there was sudden rapid gunfire and a car heading at great speed past Al, Madman and some other JC down the road. I jumped up to fire but by this point the car had already driven - because of the obstacles - into a ditch.

We surrounded the vehicle as the door burst open but someone yelled at us not to fire in taki-taki. Turns out it was a member of the JC, who had supposedly been heading to Paramaribo to kill the dictator Bourtese himself. As he jumped out, It, was obvious he was on something (pretty much all of the JC were on something), as after being hit 7 times, (twice in the neck we found out later), he acted as if he was completely fine.

He'd even walked out of the hospital we'd taken him to, that next day, talking about voodoo keeping him alive. I'd asked him how the hell he was still alive after so many hits, he simply said in his bush accent, "No time to die."

However, what had caught my attention most about that previous evening, was not the shootings, but the way the JC had reacted to something we had tried to do.

As the checkpoint seemed to be in the middle of nowhere, we wanted to check down some of the tracks that split off in the jungle just to the rear of our position. We wanted to see if there was any sign of Army vehicle movement. As we drove down we saw that the track had been used a lot by some very heavy machinery, we were a little worried about this, but not it seemed, as much as the JC where about us driving down there. There was another check point that the JC where also manning and they were not too, pleased at our arrival.

They told us to turn around immediately and go back to the VCP. As they were shouting, I looked along the track and I could see a lot of locals milling around some huts but that was about it. Then another truck from the VCP came charging down and told us we had to go back now.

I had no Idea how drugs were refined at that age, but I had seen the videos of what was happening in Columbia and the set up at that camp seemed very similar.

As we moved more and more around the jungle, we realised that some areas, were completely out of bounds to us and we just sort of accepted that Ronnie was up to something and it was probably better that we stayed out of it.

With all that aside, I was getting on very well with Ronnie and having regular tea and cake meetings with Joseph the diplomat. However, on the rare occasion that Ronnie would be around when all six of us were together, I noticed that he had an unusually large entourage around him. Something was going on, that I couldn't quite put my finger on, but I knew it wasn't good.

Mick had now fully taken on the role of "Colonel Mick" and was even getting on Ped's tits. In the bar one night when Mick was in the loo, Ped then confided in us, that actually Mick's nickname, was the lads at 2nd Rep's way of taking the piss, as this was code for his real moniker, 'Private Pike'. The rest of the night we all just kept bursting out in uncontrollable fits of laughter, as Mick, not having a clue wat was going on, only made it worse by laughing along with us.

Later that week me Al and Bill were just outside of a bar in town that did food, called the tasty bite, we nick named it the nasty bite for reasons I don't think I have to explain. As we headed back to HQ we heard a volley of gunshots and saw bits of one of the buildings fly off, we took cover and tried to locate the direction it came from, but no joy. As we did Madman just went running toward the bush firing like a lunatic. We then just followed, hard targeting to a point we thought it may have come from, firing the odd round trying to draw fire as we went, but after about half an hour of searching the bush, we found nothing.

We then went back to the YMCA and told the guy manning what was the ops (operations) room, what had happened.

He looked at us a little awkward, so we pressed him to what was going on. He then reluctantly told us that Bouterse, had now put a price on all our heads and we were now fair game for any Tom Dick or Harry to have a pop at.

This was not what any of us had signed up for and as a kick in the balls, we still hadn't had any more money.

We pressed John again, but he now told us, that there would be no bank transfer until we all got across to the west and began training the volunteers over there.

This was bollocks of course and looking in his eyes, I could see that he just desperately wanted me out of there.

That to me now, was like a red rag to a bull and just made me even more determined to stay and show him for what he really was. Given the dynamics between our two teams, we knew our money wasn't coming anytime soon and as we began to really see what was going on around us, me Al and Bill began to formulate a plan to get across to the West on our own.

Now on full drive, I began to involve myself more and more with the JC head shed and me Al and Bill began to make ourselves absolutely invaluable to the JC.

This began with more training back at the jungle camp, as we now went on to fire and manoeuvre training.

This I have to admit was a little self, preservation, as it was a little safer in the camp for the moment and we were training more men to help us, if someone did decide to have a pop at us again. Whatever the reason, although a little risky with the random shooting skills of the JC, it began to feel like we had a proper training program again.

After two days of that the JC began puffing their chests out a little and there was a lot of talk of going to kill the Tuc. I was interested now in what the men where all talking about, so that night I sat with Omleo, declining a drag on the Zeppelin of a reefer he was puffing on and with Bill helping me interpret, I tried to get him to tell me what his take on the whole situation was. He was a wily old git and kept his cards close to his chest, but I learned that things where not all what they seemed, within the JC.

It began with Omleo himself, as I asked Madman why Uncle Leo never left the camp. He looked at me and with a sadness and said, "He makes himself a prisoner."

When I asked why, he said, "Because he killed his wife with a machete." What the hell do you say to that.

As I spoke to more and more men in the camp a picture was beginning to appear, but it wasn't the simplistic one, I had been painted by John. Bill keeping his ears wide open all the time, was also helping me with that picture and as time went on, things became clearer and clearer.

The drug angle was not the main source of money and power here, there was a much bigger picture. From the Bauxite mine engineers, we found out that geologists were finding more and more signs of resources, including vast amounts of precious metals and minerals in the country.

That was where the main interest was from France, Holland, America and even now being closely watched by good old blighty.

There was also another underlying conflict, going on here and its root, was just plane racism.

As the black slaves began to take charge of their own destiny and take over the lands of Suriname. There was, more and more confrontation with the indigenous population.

These people, were known to the black community as the Tucayana and a bitter rivalry grew.

I have been to many places around the world and seen this in many forms. It angers me to see the pathetic way we deal with it in the UK, shovelled by the press, that it is only a white against black crime. So, the PC (Politically Correct) police come out and try to control free speech. All this does is create more anger, as no one can get to the route cause and ask why do people feel this way. Then we may be able to address it and ultimately erase it.

This may all seem like a conspiracy theorists rant, but I do have a point. All these actions create conflict and there is a very simple and effective art of warfare.

Divide and conquer.

Politicians and the financial elite are still doing it today and Desi Bouertese, was using it to great effect back then.

However, even this was not so simple. As we began to find out much later, the Tuc did clash with the JC, but it was Bouertese's secret army, that had been committing atrocities within the black community and then blaming it on the Tuc. This was adding fuel, to already a very hot fire.

We moved out of the camp again, no longer needing any one's permission. We now, with our fourth man, Madman and our truck, had become a little bit of a force, on our own and seemed to have the freedom to do what we wanted.

With this freedom we now began to move around the jungle as we pleased as long as it wasn't in any of Ronnie's no, go areas. We had the weapons, a large amount, of explosives a truck and a boat, so we went about, trying to put into place some sort of plan that could ultimately achieve what we had been sent to do.

This again, also helped with the not being shot at thing, as no one, not even the JC knew where we would pop up next.

As we zipped around the jungle, we saw that a lot of things were going on behind the scenes and as we pieced more and more of it together, Ronnie's Robin Hood label was beginning to look a little tainted. Also, something that hit me quite hard, was when I found out about the prostitution racket that was going on. It all came about one afternoon when we were all in the nasty bite. We were all sat out on the porch area, eating, when the children were coming out of school. As they walked by in their uniforms, there was a couple of girls who looked about 14-15, who John waved at.

They then waved back and as they did, he stuck his tongue out and darted it back and forth toward them. Al said, "What the fuck." But John said,

"Don't get on your high horse with me, I was fucking them both last, night. They just need money, like everyone else round here." Sickened as I was, I understood and it was the JC who were running it all from a building not far from the YMCA. This was the way it was here and I just needed to liven up, as to what was actually going on around me.

During this same time the relations between the two separate teams was now beginning to crumble.

Quite frankly we had no time for them, all we got was complaints about them from the locals, the police chief and some of the JC.

They weren't doing any training with the JC, not that the JC wanted them to. They had stopped patrolling the outer jungle areas and just spent their time in the Nasty Bite drinking. I admit, it was a very easy place to get comfortable and the jungle around Moengo was not, but that was the reason John had been sent home before.

With all this, I did begin to feel for the unfortunate Ped and looking back, I wish I had given him an Olive Branch and the chance to patrol with us. He did not fit in with Mick and John, he was just way too bright and would have been an absolute asset to us. I suppose he was torn because of the 2nd Rep connection and he was now unfortunately stuck with it.

John now, in a child, like, act, would completely ignore us and if possible would have sent us all back. I found out later from Ronnie that he had tried to do this, but Ronnie had stood our corner.

We were no saints either, we neglected to tell them of our acquisition of explosives and a boat. Partly because we were worried of them ruining our relationship with the locals and the missionary's, along the river, but mainly, it was out of spite. While we were all smiles when we drank together at the bar, my group began to take turns, staying awake at night.

JC with one of the local police sympathisers.

Al with one of our jungle trackers old weapons.

From front left going clockwise me, John, Bill, Al, Ped and Mick.
The night Ped told us about Private Pike.

Al with JC at a VCP.

Me and Al with Bill in foreground on river patrol.

A young JC with Bill in the Nasty Bite.

Front cover picture of Hass and me on river patrol.

JC after a weapons cleaning lesson.

JC in large sanger overlooking airstrip in Moengo.

Local villager.

Me and Bill at a VCP.

Ped and Mick on route to Moengo.

Chapter 6

All Hell

This all came to a head when John, stepped into our room at the YMCA and demanded all our weapons now, for a very important Op, then immediately turned and walked out. I looked across at Bill and Al, temper rising, and went into John's room next door. Containing my anger, I told him that we'd worked hard with the JC who had given us these weapons, we'd carefully cleaned them, and had taken forever, perfectly zeroing them to us, "These, were our weapons, why don't you go and ask Ronnie for some."

He then, still dragging on his fag and in his usual arrogant way, replied, "Ronnie has ordered me to take your weapons and you will do as your told." With complete rage running through me at this point, I was ready to smash his fucking face in. It would have been easy, I was bigger and stronger than him and I eyed Mick (who was also in the room) to see what he thought. Although I now had no respect for him at all, I hoped he still had a bit of honour in him as a soldier, I don't know why I bothered. My paranoid thoughts about him coming into our room and blasting us, so he could still live in his delusional world as the Colonel, just seemed to be confirmed. My heart now sank, as he just looked at me with a sly grin on his dopey looking face and said, "Look man, you got to understand that John's in charge, not you."

By this time, the tensions between us all, were at breaking point. Over the last week or so, sensing that John and Mick desperately wanted rid of us, my team had been on constant alert and had practically zero sleep.

I would liken it now to a Northern Ireland tour, where the people outside the fence, want to kill you, the guards on the gate want to kill you and the people in the next room on the camp, want to kill you.

I was so exhausted by all of this by now and I feel ashamed to say this, but I was thinking of killing them both, right there and then. I looked at Ped who was also in the room sat on the end of his bed. There was a man, who absolutely did not want to be around these two fucking dicks and it was painful to see. If it all kicked off, I knew Al and Bill would be there in an instant and poor Ped would probably have been mowed down with them. This wasn't what I wanted.

I stepped out of the room for a moment to calm down and join Al and Bill (who were standing outside the door, equally fuming), I then took a deep breath, turned and tried to negotiate with John, picking up his shit weapon and calmly telling him that I would speak to the JC and get his team better weapons.

That just made things ten times worse, I could tell now he was desperately trying to remain in command. John yelled at me to leave it alone, and that if I was bothered, to go and talk to Ronnie.

Shaking with rage now and almost at snapping point, I did just that, thinking if Ronnie gives me the okay, I was then going back, to beat John to death, with my bare hands.

I pleaded my case, but like a knife in the gut, Ronnie coldly told us to swap our weapons with the other team, as they needed ours for a very special operation. He told me they were going to kill Commander Thomas, leader of the Tuc, and any other Tuc that were with him.

This was now beginning to spiral way to far from what we had been tasked to do. This was an organised attack and frankly, would be no mean feat, Thomas was entrenched far west, deep in the jungle and the Tuc were supposedly jungle experts. Mick and Ped still only had the pump action shotguns they brought from French Guyenne, and John had also picked up a very rusty old Uzi 9 mm submachine gun. All were pretty limited in the environment we were working and they wouldn't stand a chance with them against the Tuc.

(We tested Johns Uzi when they had left and found that it didn't even have a firing pin and he hadn't even checked. We got it back asap).

I knew they were absolutely seething, that the JC had not deemed them fit to have theirs replaced by now and Mick and John gloated like fuck, as we handed our weapons over and we walked away with theirs.

This was a big turning point for me, the family links with Mick and the fact I liked Ped aside, this was a complete split between the two groups. That night I sat silently in my room, knowing I was never getting paid, because I wasn't following John any longer. Paranoia was now also completely taking over; John wanted us gone and now he had the better weapons. Also, over the past few days things just didn't seem right. The JC had been a bit off with us and they seemed to want to contain us within the town itself. It even seemed like

Ronnie was no longer on our side, and I had not spoken to, or even seen Joseph, in the last week.

We now worried that both, Ronnie and John, were planning on, dealing with us. Again, we got very little sleep that night and then these feelings were enhanced the next day, by the arrival of another Legionnaire, Gary, who had been on route from the UK, for the past two days.

(Gary; we nicknamed 'the unluckiest soldier in the world', was in his late 20s and also former 2nd Rep. He looked like your average GI Joe with short, dark hair and a stocky build).

We met him in the YMCA, where we shook his hand and tried to be as accommodating as we could, as he'd done nothing wrong. Immediately he could sense something odd with the whole situation. He then swiftly went off with John, Mick, and Ped, where he was given a weapon and briefed on what his mission was.

He was already fully kitted out, (like a Foreign Legion soldier) as Mick had told him there was nothing in the jungle. This just compounded the paranoia, as there was now four of them, all with better weapons.

Luckily, they all left that same night, knowing what the mission was, I almost feared for Mick, Ped, and the now unfortunate Gary.

After they had gone, the atmosphere between the three of us, was deflated. This whole thing seemed a complete disaster. We now sadly all thought about getting out of there ASAP. I went to speak to Ronnie again, who had just got back from making sure the others had set off okay.

I felt awkward, but told him that we thought it was now time to leave. We had not been paid as promised by John and there was now nothing here for us to stay for.

There was then, another big switch in Ronnie's attitude towards us from the days before. It was suddenly like he was our best friend again. He begged us all to stay, telling us he would come to some arrangement on payment. Ronnie had been paying us living expenses in local money, which was a fortune to the local people, but it wasn't enough to go back to the UK with, and definitely not worth being here for.

There was also something that Ronnie had said that threw me when we discussed the rift between the two teams, and the mission to take out Commander Thomas. When I mentioned it, he had given me a sly smile and said: "Commander Thomas is a long way away. I think, maybe, they don't come back."

That next day we, where in the YMCA, discussing our options. Ronnie said he wanted us to stay, but everything felt wrong, and I believed that nobody was ever getting paid. There was also a heightening tension between us and the JC, but I still could not understand why.

I know Ronnie had been all smiles, but the term smiling assassin had jumped into my head a few times. Even Madman was avoiding us and we started to fear, we would be killed at any time.

Then that evening one of Ronnie's main men burst in and ordered us to go immediately to see him in the air tower. He then quickly disappeared and we all looked at each other with dread. As we exited the building and headed towards the air field, there was a stillness throughout the town; a lack of the JC anywhere. We had been patrolling the Moengo area, just to keep us busy and it had been like this all day.

As we reached the edge of the air strip, we saw a light in the control tower in the distance and nervously headed towards it. Already the hairs on the back of my neck were standing on end.

Walking across that open space, we felt incredibly vulnerable, but I felt that if we had walked along the edge of the trees and entered in the back way, it would have looked very suspicious to Ronnie.

As we got closer, I wished we had.

From the light in and around the tower, I could now make out 20 or more JC, all heavily armed and looking prepared for a fire fight. We were now at the point where we couldn't run, but far enough away that I could speak in a hushed voice to Al and Bill, who-sensing what I had, fanned out to either side of me. As I was about to tell them to slip their safety catches off, I heard the faint clicks of them doing so. Then I quietly told them, "If the JC start firing, hit the deck, take as many of them down as you can, and then make a dash for the tree line." Given the shit weapons we now had, we didn't stand a chance.

As we walked closer to the light, with our senses heightening at every step, something happened between us that night, something I will never forget. Despite the fear, I was now overcome with an unbelievable pride. Throughout all of this, Al and Bill had never flinched and stood solid with me at that moment, ready to die. Even now, there's a lump in my throat remembering it.

As we made our way towards the JC, the closer we got, the less likely I felt they would open up on us. Although they greatly outnumbered us, we strode toward them with purpose and without fear, it was now they, who looked like crumbling. There was definitely something wrong, but soldiers know to fire from a distance. If they were going to shoot us, they would have done it by now.

We finally reached the control room and as we entered, I clocked Madman on the other side of the glass walls encasing us. He had this look on his face, one of sympathy. It seemed that he wanted no part of what was going on here.

Ronnie didn't greet us in his usual friendly way and stayed seated in a chair, next to a tape recorder. After an awkward pause, he told us he wanted us to listen carefully and pressed play.

Two men's voices could be heard and while garbled, I saw Bill's eyes widen, he had sussed who it was, immediately. Me and Al were a little slower to follow but with a cold shiver now running down my back, I heard Johns voice and he was talking about assassinating Ronnie.

The other person in the conversation I found out to be a representative of Bouterse and they were in the Surinamese embassy in Holland. It sounded like someone else was in the room, with the movement of chairs and greetings, but they never spoke.

The recording had been made by Dutch Intelligence many months before, but I did not know when it had been given to Ronnie.

Ronnie stared at me intently, as I listened to the tape. When it was finished, he asked me bluntly if I knew anything about this. I stood there for a moment speechless, watching fingers get tighter around triggers. Realising the gravity of the situation, I took another of the many deep breaths I had taken here, stared him right back in the eye and told him, "Absolutely not."

Ronnie looked at us all curiously, searching our eyes for something, then gave me a big smile, jumped up, and in his classic switch of moods. Gave us all one of his big hugs and said, "I believe you."

The whole atmosphere changed in an instant. The JC relaxed, some smiled and even shook our hands and I saw Madman through the glass; his eyes welling up, with the biggest smile I've ever seen.

As we walked back into town (it was definitely beer time after that), we tried to piece together everything that had happened over the past few weeks: the mood of the JC, why Ronnie had kept our group separated and was never alone with any of us, John's disappearances in Holland, my gut instinct when I first met him and how our dislike of him had probably saved all our lives.

Something else though, was now bothering me, it was Bill. Something wasn't right in his body language and the way he knew who it was on the garbled recording straight away, was playing on me.

He knew something I didn't and as we got well out of sight of the JC along the tree line, I pulled him. Getting right in his face I said, "What the fucks going on Bill?" Al had noticed it too and before Bill had a chance so say he didn't know what we were on about,

Al said, "No fucking bullshit Bill, we need to know right now."

Bill, was the other guy in the room.

Looking at both of us, he then bleated out, "I didn't know what he was going to say, I was just there as back up."

He then gave us an elaborate story of how it all came about and that he didn't think John was serious. We didn't completely believe him, but having been through what we all had together, he was one of us now and as such was under our protection. As we continued back, he knew he was seriously in the dog house. Jesus, I thought, how wrong could that have all gone, if Bill had said something in that recording. We carried on to the Nasty Bite, had a few beers and some food, all on Bills tab and then went back to the YMCA.

As we sat talking about what had gone on since we got here, all still trying to connect the dots and with my mind a little clearer now. I couldn't help but think with a slight pang of sadness, mixed with a bit of satisfaction about Mick and the others who had gone with John.

The next couple of days were spent rebuilding our relationship with the JC, and after a visit to Omleo, we acquired some proper weapons again. Al got his Minimi LMG, and me and Bill took FALs. Bill had also managed to get himself a really nice sniper night sight and like a kid in a toy shop, was exited as hell at the thought of playing with it. We also took some of the shotguns, sawed off the barrels and shoulder stock and slung them as backup-weapons for close jungle combat.

As a little trophy and with the firing pin back in, I also had Johns Uzi as a side arm back up.

We were now all tooled up like a small army, if anybody wanted to take us out now, I thought, good luck to them. We had another river trip to check on the villagers and missionaries, as there had still been a little trouble with the 'Tuc' stealing stuff. While everything seemed calmer, I was still wondering what would happen with John if and when he returned.

Then the other team's situation went from bad to worse. We again, with Madman, had just come back from patrol, up river and were tying up the boat. When two JC arrived in a truck, told us to jump in and we then sped off back to the YMCA.

On arrival, there was a big commotion in the dining hall. Joseph, the diplomat, led me in and Al and Bill were told to wait outside. Al gave me a look that said he would be straight in if any trouble should arise. Especially since I wasn't allowed to take in my weapons.

Ronnie was sat at the top table, flanked by his two bodyguards. The three of them were the only ones armed and Ronnie had his shiny pistol on display. Also, at the table were two intelligence officers, French and Dutch, Hass (the police chief), a couple of prominent locals from around the town, and half a dozen others I had never seen before.

Joseph sat me besides him, opposite the French Intelligence Officer, who was obviously seething about something. I had seen and spoke to him a few times around the YMCA, as he was the Liaison officer, from French Guyenne. There had previously been an incident where we were all heading back into the YMCA after being in town with Mick, John, and Ped. Mick and Ped were now a little worse for wear from the drink. So, started joking around, acting as all 20-something year old soldiers do, kicking the doors open and pretending to clear the room.

The Liaison had been there and Bill had overheard him calling them children. When he had gone over to the Officer to try and clear things up, Bill was told that they should not be wearing their French Legionnaire uniforms. Legionnaires were based in Kourou in French Guyenne next door and if

Mick and Ped continued to wear their uniforms it would look as if the French had a military involvement in Suriname. This would create problems for the French government, who were already struggling with instability in French Guyenne.

Bill, in his usual diplomatic way, tried to help him and warn Mick and Ped, but even when they had sobered up the next day, they simply refused to listen.

My team had adapted our uniforms from the beginning; as a 'Brits on Tour' label was not a good one. Also, after the first time we had been shot at, we began to dress a little more like the JC to blend in.

As I entered the room it was manic and filled with shouting in various languages. Joseph then called for quiet, which everyone obeyed, sitting down. He remained standing, and said, "Please, can everyone in the room converse in English for…" pointing to me, "his benefit and explain what is, going on."

Ronnie was the first to speak. He told me, in his distinct way: "John and the others have done very bad thing. They go to jungle, to kill Commander Thomas, they get very lost, attack army post, and kill soldiers in beds."

What, What, I couldn't get my head round what he had just said, why would they do that, shit this was bad. We all knew Ronnie had been using our presence as a lever, to push the government into calling a ceasefire. This had been going on almost since we arrived, and peace negotiations had even started about democratic elections being held in Paramaribo. This was all favoured by the French and the Dutch, hence their presence at the table and was the very thing I had come here, to try and achieve.

What had actually happened, was that Ronnie had sent them on the Op hoping the Tuc would do what he wanted to do and kill them all. However, the map reading element was sadly lacking in the team and they had got completely lost. As they wandered around the jungle, they had stumbled on a, small army post. Then Mick, out of frustration had bullied the others into attacking it.

I sat stunned for a second, not knowing what the hell to say, when the French intelligence officer stood up. He then told me venomously that "This incident may cause a delay in the Arianne Rocket Launch," this was in French Guyana next door, "to send a communication satellite into space. This could lose the French Government billions of dollars, as a potential full-scale war in Suriname could arise from what they had done."

The officer then started a personal attack on the former Legionnaires, which Joseph quickly cut off by asking him to sit down.

Joseph then looked over to the Dutch Intelligence Officer, who stood and explained why they were worried the conflict might escalate. He said, "A large amount of the population in The Netherlands and Paramaribo were very pro-Ronnie and had been very sympathetic to his plight. However, this incident could completely dislodge that trust, as the ceasefire had been very clear, and the soldiers killed (who had families back in the capital) had not been on a war footing."

After this had all been explained to me, I sat there, shoulders stooped, completely stunned and not knowing what the hell to do. Joseph then put his hand on my shoulder, reassuring me that everything was okay, and said to the room, "We must now decide what to, do when John returns."

They then, all discussed calmly and openly what was to happen next, although the two intelligence officers, now kept quiet.

The consensus was to kill them all and send their bodies back to Paramaribo, this would explain that they weren't with Ronnie. This was the only way to ensure that the ceasefire would continue, and to keep peace negotiations going.

I was absolutely floored, by how coldly and efficiently this was planned. Even Joseph, who I had tagged as the calm, reasonable mediator, agreed with the majority.

Joseph then halted the discussion and turned to me, to ask my thoughts on the fate of four lives, one of whom I still had family ties with, back in the UK.

My throat was screaming for moisture, as I thought desperately what to say. I tried to pick my words carefully, but felt I had to be honest, as there were many people in that room far cleverer than me and would see through a lie instantly.

I then tried to explain that I thought Mick, Ped, and Gary had just been blindly following John, not knowing his ulterior motives. Many in the room knew that Mick especially, wasn't the brightest and when I argued this there were a few smiles of agreement, which then made it easier for me to continue. I asked them to spare the lives of Mick, Ped and Gary and to let me explain the situation to them on their return, then the JC could escort them to the border of French Guyenne. With each word, I thought I was digging my own grave, in that room, within minutes, I aged 20 years.

After I finished, I sat quietly, looking around the room, trying to read the faces of the people around me, I just couldn't tell what they were thinking. Joseph simply thanked me and asked if I could please leave the room. I then awkwardly stood up and left.

Once the door closed behind me, Bill and Al jumped up to ask me what the fuck was going on. I took my weapons back from Al, and told them I would explain once we were outside.

As we walked around the building I relayed the events and what was going to happen to all of them, if they didn't play ball.

Bill was as cold as the men back in the dining hall (he'd always hated the three of them and how they belittled him because he wasn't 2nd Rep). Al was a bit more sympathetic, especially for poor Gary, who had only just turned up and was now about to be executed.

By the time we walked back to the dining hall, the room was now emptying and Joseph beckoned me over. He told me that I was allowed to speak to Mick on their return. He said, "If he listens, okay. If he doesn't, it will be very bad for him and his friends." I then asked about John, to which he replied with a simple movement of his hand slicing across his throat (that seems a bit dramatic, but that's what he did).

I now desperately needed to have a long serious private chat, with both of the Int officers.

Ronnie had sent a large group of JC to go and look for Johns team and It took a few days for them to find them and get them back. While we were waiting for their return, 'all hell' broke loose in the jungle and the retaliations began.

Local JC sympathisers outside of Moengo, were now being regularly tortured and killed and we were having to hard target everywhere as we didn't know who would now take a pot shot at us. Those stupid bastards had caused so much trouble, that our lives were now in constant danger.

On the afternoon of the next day, we were told that a force of Tuc had descended on the village where the American missionaries were, and were threatening to kill them unless those responsible for the soldier shootings were handed over.

We didn't need to be told, but we couldn't get there quickly enough in the boat. There were two aircraft going in and out of Moengo all the time and a BN Islander, overhead wing, twin prop aircraft, was sat at the airstrip. So, we raced over to the Nasty Bite, dragged the pilot out and told him to fly us straight to the missionary village. He didn't argue, but as he took off, he immediately banked the opposite way to where we were headed. I grabbed his shoulder and shouted, "You're going the wrong fucking way." He told me that everything was okay, and continued around back onto the correct flight path. As I looked out, I noticed something in the jungle out of the window that he had avoided flying over. This finally confirmed to me what was going on here, with this and another aircraft, a twin otter and the two Spanish speaking Americans flying them. I really could not ignore what I was seeing any more and what I was seeing, was that Ronnie, was not so much a Robin Hood, but more of a Pablo Escobar.

We then flew fast and low over the jungle.

We had the side door open, and Al and Bill squat down on the edge with guns pointing out jamming their shoulders in the door frame. As we flew toward the missionaries' hospital, we saw a red pickup truck and lots of armed men milling around, who, on seeing the aircraft, ran back to the truck and sped away.

We didn't fire on our first pass, as we needed to identify the target, and were thrown a few times as the Tuc didn't match up to their description. We quickly looped around, during which time, they began firing on us. That was all Al needed and he opened up, Bill and I followed suit. The bullets just started to shred the back of their vehicle and I saw one of them definitely hit and almost flop out of the back, when it disappeared under the jungle canopy.

A lot of bullets had come our way, but as I found in the Falklands, it's really difficult to take out an aircraft with small arms fire unless it was very well coordinated cross fire and we didn't get a scratch. Fair play to the drug running ballsy pilot.

We flew around for another 10 minutes or so, but had lost them.

We then landed, and legged it over to the hospital where they were trying to treat a young villager with his face smashed in and multiple stab wounds. The hospital there, couldn't cope with those sorts of injuries, so we flew him back to the Dutch hospital in Moengo, which had better surgical facilities. I don't know whether he lived or died.

All a bit depressed that night and sick as fuck of hard targeting around Moengo, we went out to one of the local villages in the jungle, where Al had struck up a relationship with one of the teachers. I know this sounds bad, but me and Bill would keep her dad chatting with some ciggies and a couple of bottles of beer, while Al whispered sweet nothing in her ear, if you know what I mean. Once all the whispering was over and we said our goodbyes to the father, we then made our way back to the truck.

As we were about to get in, we heard gunshots and felt something hit our bare, arms and faces. It was weird, it stung like hell and felt like someone had fired fine gravel at us, with a very powerful catapult. Automatically we hit the deck and turned to the direction of fire, where we could see what looked like two shotgun barrels poking out of a window way in the distance. None of us were taking any shit now and we fired and manoeuvred right at them as fast as we could.

As me and Al approached the door, Bill ran around the rear. I kicked the door open and put in a couple of rounds. Then Al ran in and seeing a guy at the back door turning to fire again, double tapped him in the chest. He dropped and as we ran through we could now see another guy in the rear garden, who had dropped his weapon and was now pleading with Bill not to shoot him.

By now the rest of the small village had come out carefully to see what was going on. Al's lady, seeing what we had done gave him a look that said there would be no more whispering and the rest of the village became very aggressive toward us. Not really understanding now what was going on, we thought better to leave. So, we quickly grabbed the other guy, threw him in the truck and took him back to Moengo for questioning.

When we got back to HQ the JC already knew what was going on and pulled the guy out of the truck. When they started to question him, I wished we had left the poor bastard in the village. He was one of the local villagers and was desperately just trying to feed his family, so him and his friend had tried to take some of Bouterse's reward and have a go at us. I just couldn't take all this in now, what the hell did they think they could do, firing buck shot from about 150 metres away. It was pathetic and as things got heated, I got angry, not at the poor bastard now getting a severe beating, but at the JC who were inflicting it. "That's enough," I said as Al and Bill tried to protect him. Al then said, "Look he's our fucking prisoner, so we will deal with it." We then shoved him back in the truck and headed off back to the village.

He was now in a right state, crying, begging and had pissed all over the seat, thinking we were going to shoot him. We couldn't get him out of the truck quick enough and dropped him off on the outskirts of the village, as we thought there would be a few more shotguns out by now.

Looking at him stood in the road, through the rear, view mirrors, as we drove away, this whole place was now beginning to grind me down. Yes, they had tried to kill us, but we all didn't think it was right that we had taken one of them out. They had just done it out of desperation and didn't really stand a chance. As we drove back to Moengo in complete silence, we all knew, that this was the beginning of the end, of our time in Suriname.

Chapter 7

Back in Moengo

We went straight to the Nasty Bite, with the attitude of 'fuck the lot of you!' We would have been straight out of there, if it wasn't for the fact that we wanted to try and save Ped, Gary and – I hate to say it now– even Mick.

Sitting in the bar that night while the drinks flowed, we discussed getting out of there, talking complete bollocks.

"We could come back with a shitload of guys and take over the whole fuckin' country," said Al.

I agreed. "Just one call to Dirty Delta and I'll have a full troop – a whole platoon – of very nasty Paratroopers, chomping at the bit!"

Drunken banter, but it got me through the night, and at least we were laughing together again – something we hadn't done in a while.

Thinking about the other team, I knew they would never have developed the camaraderie and bond that me, Al, Bill and even Madman had made. Madman – who sadly didn't drink and was on lemonade – just sat there looking perplexed at these three drunken bums talking shit. When we left the bar slightly wobbly, that night, we couldn't be arse'd to hard target and would have almost welcomed a firefight. I couldn't have hit a barn door, but never mind.

Back at HQ, a few of the JC were still hanging around talking to a couple of the 'schoolgirls' and there was still a bit of tension from earlier. Again, I thought, *Bring it on!* But unless there were 20 of them, they didn't have the bottle. Shooting someone in the back, though – that was more their style. And now, with a raised price on our heads, sending a couple of European soldiers back to Paramaribo in a box could make them a lot of money and possibly even national heroes.

Lying, still slightly drunk on my pit with me weapon laid beside me that night, was the worst time for me in this whole saga. It wasn't because of all that was happening around me – but what was not happening. I now seemed to have no drive or sense of purpose for what I was doing here. I'd had a mission – and as soon as we'd arrived, it seemed that that mission had gone completely on the back burner. This was not how I operated. If you asked some of the senior officers I served under, later in life, they would tell you that I drove them up the wall with my persistence and would never be told I couldn't do something. I had tried and tried to make things happen here, but I had been held back by forces completely out of my control. I began again, to think seriously about our drunken ideas in the bar. However, that would have needed not only the green light from the French – which I think they would have given, but also from back home, which I know they would not. Not on the scale I was thinking, anyway.

We stayed out of Moengo roaming the jungle up river, all the next day, to see if things would calm down a bit; still waiting for something else to kick off while we waited for the others. But us chasing off the truck up at the missionary's place and Al double tapping one of the villagers who had just tried to kill us, seemed to be making everyone think twice about having a go, now, and it stayed quiet all day.

Then, that evening, the moment of truth came. We were called outside the YMCA, because the JC had found John and the others wandering the jungle, lost, and we were told that they would be arriving by truck shortly. They all still had no idea, of the mess they were in.

It's hard to describe how I was feeling, as I stood waiting outside the YMCA that evening. There was no single emotion, but a wave of them constantly flowing back and forth through me. I can't compare it with being shot at, or anything else that had happened to me there, but it reminds me of incidents later in life.

Within the military and further down the road in my career, I had done well over a thousand parachute jumps, mostly freefall – and in all those times, I had three malfunctions, of varying severity, one of them very severe. Each time it happened, it seemed like things went into slow motion; but the reality is, that your senses become extremely heightened and you deal with things at an incredible speed. As the trucks pulled up, I now seemed to see and feel absolutely everything around me, in slow motion.

Mick jumped out immediately and came bounding over to me. "Fuckin' hell, man! You shoud'a seen us, man! We killed 'em all, man. They didn't know what fuckin' hit 'em!" he bragged.

I stared at him in disbelief as he continued with his story in a heightened state – almost a caricature of himself and how he always spoke. It was as if he was trying to ingratiate himself with me, acting as if we were best buddies again. I realised that his senses were heightened, too – but his were out of pure fear. He then began gabbling incoherently.

"Hang on, Mick." I tried to calm him down and get him to listen to what I was saying, deadly serious. But he was confused by how I was dealing with him, so I grabbed his shoulders, stared him straight in the eyes and told him urgently, "Listen to me and do exactly what I say!"

As I was trying to explain, Ped and Gary (who had been overly quiet) left the truck and looked nervously at the number of JC now surrounding them. They could see that something here was very, very wrong.

John also knew, especially when several JC had grabbed his weapon and knocked him to the ground.

Ped and Gary, still not understanding what was going on, were about to raise their weapons, but Al and Bill shouted at them, "No! Stop. Stay cool!"

"It's just John they want!" Al cried.

Mick looked around, to see John being hauled to his feet. I now shook Mick urgently by the shoulders, shouting, "Mick! Listen to me now! Or we are *all dead*!"

I could feel more JC appearing, and I was expecting us all to be shot at any time.

"You fuckin' idiots…" I tried desperately to explain to Mick the trouble they had caused by killing the soldiers.

Although it was clear that fear was coursing through him, I could see that it just wasn't sinking in. I changed tack and told him quickly about the tape recording. This was a lot simpler for him to understand.

Then, something inside Mick – anger, or more likely, the fear – made him run over and smash John's head with the butt of his rifle while John was being held with his arms behind his back. John went down to his knees with the first blow and blood spurted from around his left eye. Mick would have kept on bashing his head in; but by now Al and Bill, along with some of the JC, were pulling him away.

I grabbed Mick again and could now see in his eyes, that he would do exactly as I said.

"Look," I told him. "Take it easy and you, Ped, and Gary will be escorted back to French Guyana, immediately. But…" and this was a big but, "… you have to give up your weapons right now!"

I knew this would be the hardest part. It would leave them incredibly vulnerable, but I told them, calmly, "This is the only way you'll get out of here alive."

It was one of those short moments that felt like an eternity.

Mick, now completely withering away, agreed and gave me his rifle. Ped couldn't give his up quickly enough. We found out later that he had actually tried to stop Mick charging into the army post and killing them. He knew what they had done was completely fucking crazy. Again, I felt for this poor lad, who had just been drawn in with a couple of arseholes because of his cap badge. Gary, then, seeing that he had no choice, relented and handed his weapon to Al.

Castro – the little shit bag – then appeared and shouted at them, "Get in the trucks! Go!"

With Mick and the rest now unarmed and defenceless, the JC began to jostle them to the trucks with a bit more authority.

Just before they left, I walked over to Mick who was sitting wide-eyed in the back of a truck and held his arm. reassuringly. "Mate," I faked, "everything will be okay," I told him. "I'll ring you in a couple of days, once you're back in England. See if you're alright."

He didn't say anything – just looked at me with empty eyes and a blank expression.

As they pulled away, I watched them deflated and scared, I tried to keep eye contact with Mick but he looked away from me. I couldn't stand John, but it was now Mick I held in the most contempt, he was the worst type of soldier. He had never seen any action and all he had wanted to do, was say he had killed someone. If, it had to be people sleeping, so be it. There would be others I would meet over the years, who had that same attitude, but they would be quickly weeded out. Mostly through physical selection, then others later, as their cowardice was unravelled. I stood there fixed on him, until the truck disappeared out of Moengo and headed onwards, toward the border.

There was now the issue of John. He had now been bound and thrown into the back of a truck. He didn't say anything, just sat there in silence. Then as the JC were loaded up around him, Ronnie with a look in his eyes that I had never seen before, suddenly appeared and we were told to follow in another truck. Understanding now exactly what Ronnie wanted, we then headed out of town, towards the jungle.

We pulled up abruptly a couple of kilometres from the town. There, John was hauled from the wagon and pulled towards a tree, where he was tied. Now, I am not a religious man, but I couldn't help but look up at the stars at that moment to try and find some answer, for what I knew was about to happen.

We were then asked to exit the truck. "Go – talk to him."

Grim-faced, we went over to John. Crouching down, Al lit a fag and gave it to him.

With the fag hanging in his mouth, and still sat tied to the tree, John asked me, "What's going to happen to me?"

I'm not sure why, maybe I wanted to put him at ease, but I told him, "The JC are just going to question you about the tape recording. If you tell the truth, you'll be okay."

I just didn't want him to be afraid.

As we turned and walked back toward the trucks. I could see that Al was sick to his stomach and I knew why. Death in combat is one thing; execution is another.

He looked at me and said, "I'm sorry mate, but I want no part in this."

I couldn't help but just hug him as tightly as I could. This fearless bastard, had a heart as big as the ocean; but as I held him, I knew we had to see this through or we could all be tied to that tree.

It then went silent. Everything went dark, and in the jungle that night, the shots rang out.

The firing stopped momentarily and John, still alive, tried to speak, his punctured lungs gurgling as he gasped to say something with his last breath. I watched, as one more shot went directly to his head – and then, he was gone.

That night will live with me forever.

John's body was left there tied to the tree, for the jungle animals to feed on. Then, all in complete silence, we and the JC took the trucks back to the YMCA.

As we stepped off the truck, Ronnie was waiting. I needed to find out what our options were now, but mostly, I needed to know what John had been up to. His kit was still in the other wagon, and I grabbed it. For a moment, Ronnie seemed as if he was going to stop me; but looking at the three of us, now, he thought better of it.

The kit the other team had left behind had already been ransacked by the JC days before. A couple of them were now sporting some nice Legion-issue Ray-Ban sunglasses and new cameras. Me and the boys had already been through most of it, before them. All we wanted was information; but John had been careful to take anything important with him. Now we had his kit and a notebook from his person, we prayed it would shed some light on this whole shitstorm.

As we went through it all, frustratingly, it still gave us no clear answers. However, we now had his bank details and contacts diary. Since we were about six hours or so behind Europe time wise. it wouldn't be long before we could make a morning call to Rajin and a few others to get some answers.

We had a few fitful hours' sleep, with one of us always awake, and as soon as we could, we made our way to the radio telephone tower in the centre of Moengo.

Rajin was our first port of call, but it seemed that he had already been told about what had happened to John and I could tell by his voice that he was absolutely shitting himself. This was a man who would be careful not to bullshit any of us, now.

It seemed there was a grain of truth in what John had initially told us, but the figures he had given us – and the *when* anyone would actually get any of the money they had been promised had been – let's say – a little distorted.

After we had spoken to various sources, it seemed that John had been paid a small amount upfront for recruiting everyone – and we had been given all, we would ever get. Carrying on with the Op out to the west was way out of John's league – and he could never have got away with slotting Ronnie; not without help, anyway. It seemed that he had just been trying to get more money upfront for something he did not have the skills to complete.

It was now clear that all he'd wanted to do was to get enough material for the newspapers so he could tell another tale about his mercenary exploits in South America. This, it seems, he was quite content to do from the comfort of the Nasty Bite in Moengo, while we were all out there risking our lives as unpaid fillers – only there to stoke the fire of his ego.

After John's death, things remained quiet on the 'being attacked' front. A day and a half after the others had been kicked out, I rang Mick's girlfriend's flat to see if he was there. I did genuinely want to see if they were safe and that they'd all got back okay – but I also knew that if they hadn't, it was very unlikely that we would, either.

Mick answered the phone.

While I can't remember exactly what he said, I remember how he said it. He was completely off with me, as if it was somehow all my fault – but deep down, I could only hear shame in his voice. I understood why. There he was – one minute, 'Colonel Mick', barking orders, saying he was the 'King of Suriname' – the next, kicked out of the country with his tail between his legs for a complete and utter fuck-up.

Stupidly, I felt hurt, I'd been expecting more of a thank you for saving his and all the others' lives. He had no idea of the risks we all took, trying to defend him – and the amount of retaliation we had to endure. Shooting soldiers, you were not at war with – while they slept – was not something I would brag about. The truth is, he was just too fucking dumb to realise what he had done. A thank you never came, and I never spoke to Mick again.

That same day, Castro came rushing into the YMCA, shouting, "You must come! Many Tuc are coming! You must go kill them! Now!"

A bit of R&R on washday by the river.

Another very young JC.

Al with Bill's new toy.

Eric from the French TV crew with Edward.

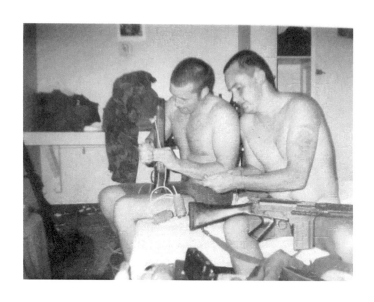

Me and Bill making IEDs (Improvised Explosive Devices).

Me taking 5 at the JC's jungle camp.

Me and Al with his new-found side arm, a Mac 10 machine pistol,
in the Nasty Bite.

Al and me taking time out in the sports bar.

Pat Baker leaving Cayenne Airport.

Ronnie with John, just weeks before he had him executed.

The YMCA dining hall.

The weapons haul from the ambush.

Front from left to right, Ped, John and Mick.
Rear Me, Bill, Edward and Al.

Chapter 8

The Clearer Picture

There was a ditch just to our left, and through instinct, the three of us ran as fast as we could, zig zagging as we went, waiting for the inevitable pain that comes with a bullet. We made it to the ditch and dived in, still all unbelievably, unharmed. We then pointed our weapons toward the JC ready to fire, absolutely furious at them for turning on us after all that we had done for them. But as I pulled them into my sights in the darkness, about to fire, I could hear that the JC, had stopped firing and now in silhouette against the sky, I could see their weapons were clearly aimed directly into the air.

What the fuck was going on.

Then one of the JC saw us in the ditch and pointed us out to Ronnie, who asked us calmly, "What are you doing?" None of us had an answer and Ronnie just broke into laughter, along with the rest of the JC. We found out why they had done this, much later.

With us now high on adrenalin, the whole place was a party, but like on our arrival at the sports bar, I knew this could quickly change. We went to speak to Ronnie and told him that this was the JC's celebration, and we just wanted to go somewhere quiet. He understood, and said he would see us in the morning. Ronnie also knew how things could go with the JC, and encouraged them to all continue at the jungle camp where he would send some entertainment (local working girls and booze).

Sitting back in our room, we now had to decide what we were going to do next, and as we talked into the night, the argument for leaving got ever stronger.

Surprisingly, we all slept better that night than, we had in a long time, without any fear and late into the next day.

When Ronnie came he had his money bag as promised and again Bill had a look through. Seeing Bill was not impressed, Ronnie then shouted to a JC who brought over another large sack filled with what looked like fine shiny sand. Bill knew straight away, it was gold. Ronnie controlled the mining in his area of occupation and on the river at Langa-tabbetje that's what was dredged. He told us it was all he had and again, said he would get more if we stayed. I knew what he was doing, he was keeping the carrot just close enough to try and sway us. To him we, after what we did last night, were now a very powerful stick he had to swing and he would have much more leverage, at the negotiating table, with us around.

Thinking he had us by the balls, his jaw dropped when we thanked him, took the money and gold and told him we were leaving. Looking back now, yes, there was, so much opportunity to make a hell of a lot of money in that country. With control of all the vast recourses the country had and bringing back Dutch, French and English contractors, protected by your own little army, the sky would have been the limit. However, I had read a lot of stories about the same thing in Africa, with Mad Mike Hoar, Colonel Callan and the

142

rest. All of which, did not end well and with me just a mere corporal, it didn't end to well for Hitler either.

I was still only 24 years old and I knew my limits, I was going home to try and kick start my life back there. This place would always be in turmoil and you never knew, I could end up back there as a grown up some day. So, if the Suriname people ever read this and would like a change, give me a call, I still know a lot of very nasty Paratroopers.

Mick and the rest had got back swiftly and without incident, but now we didn't think it would be that easy. We wasted no time, packed our bags, commandeered one of the young JC as navigator, jumped in our truck and drove off. We didn't even say goodbye to Madman or Hass, couldn't have stood the tears.

We now had to take a different route from the way we came. This meant traveling way down south east, to the island of Langa-tabbetje, and the small JC outpost there. Then travel by canoe, back up along the river covered by a couple of small islands to St-Jean at the southern part of St Laurent, well away from Albina camp.

As we drove, there was now an unbelievable feeling of relief and it showed in all our faces. With money in our pockets, we felt like we were off on some jolly. It felt good just to take in the scenery and appreciate, just how beautiful it could be here. We were still tooled up to the teeth and felt pretty confident as we lazily made our way on a small dirt road through the jungle.

We didn't get to the island till later that evening, but the JC who manned it, knew what we had done and there was a little bit of hero worship when we got there. They already had some food on the go of, Cayman (small alligator) and (Rot tie) large Guinea Pig with a bit of rice and the beers where chilling in the fridge, powered by a very noisy generator.

After we had eaten, Al, god bless him, volunteered to go back to St Laurent first, to see the lay of the land that night, while me and Bill would wait for a call to see if all was okay. As he climbed into the canoe, we shook his hand wishing him luck and as he headed off in the canoe with the boatman, he then pulled off the most ridiculous Fred Scuttle (Benny Hill) salute ever, as he floated away.

Bill had been a big surprise to me on this job, with his fluent French and his knowledge of explosives and pretty much everything else, he had been an unbelievable asset and will always be a friend. But as I watched Al disappear in the darkness, I knew that I could not have got through this without him. His bravery was unquestionable, but it was his honesty and his sense of what was right and what was wrong, when mine was failing, that kept us all, on the right path.

Dare I say it, "I love the ugly fucker."

Me and Bill didn't get much sleep that night in our hammocks, but that was just due to us chin wagging by the fire and relaying the airplane incident and the ambush to our captive audience. It was the next morning before we got the call. It was strange hearing his voice at the end of a telephone line and not on a radio. He told us that the French police were waiting as expected. They had hand cuffed him to a radiator for a while but otherwise everything was fine and they just wanted us out of the country sharpish.

So, we jumped into the next available boat, very similar to the one we arrived in and set off. It seemed strange that even though we were crossing in broad daylight, I felt none of the pressure I had felt in the darkness on the way in and as

144

I watched the animals scurry about the banks of the river, it just felt like a safari boat ride.

In no time, we hit the shore in St-Jean, and handed our weaponry to the boatman just as we saw the police heading toward us. Even with their hands resting on the top of their pistols, they were very cordial, only asking if we were unarmed. We told them, we now were as the boatman was now halfway back to the other side and they then, put us into a Police van. They drove us into St Laurent and stopped at the police station, picked up Al and then we all headed immediately to Cayenne. The journey was very subdued and we said very little as we looked now out of the windows watching the scenery in reverse. It seemed a lifetime ago from when we first came here, I felt very calm and found myself drifting off.

Now pulling up to the police station in Cayenne, things changed.

There was a number of film news crews outside and they swamped the van as we pulled up. As we got out, we covered our faces as best we could and the police did a good job of keeping them at bay. We then quickly got into the station and as we were ushered in, it now all went very formal. After our names were taken at the desk and our equipment confiscated, we were then taken to the cells, three next to each other and the doors were locked behind us. As I sat on the bed listening to the commotion die down outside, I wondered what the hell would happen now.

About half an hour later, the doors of the cell opened quickly, but no one came in, instead there was a shout for us all to come out. I now expected a, police beating and stepped out ready for a fight, but I just saw Al and Bill stood there like me, fists clenched.

One of the cops then called from along the corridor and said that if we wanted a drink, to go with him. We followed as he took us into the station kitchen, with half a dozen other officers sat in there. It had a little bar and a TV up on a shelf in the corner, that they were all watching. He then asked us to sit down and if we wanted a beer. Now this was weird, but things got weirder.

We were now getting on famously with the cops. They were bringing us all sorts of weapons that they had confiscated and asked if we could strip them and check they were safe. Al was now in his element; a Gaulouise in his mouth and a beer in in hand, giving the frogs weapon lessons. Bill was also in full flow, talking politics and the current dislike of the French government. I just sort of sat there, looking at them, content and thinking how far away from that night on the airfield we were.

We would be getting the plane back to Paris soon, so they let us clean up as best we could, and we got all of our kit back and I mean all of our kit. The van then arrived to take us to the airport and the senior rank of the escort party came in. However, an argument then started between him and the custody Sergeant. Bill (translating) told us that the cops in the station wanted us to stay to watch the evening news, but the other cop was complaining that the 747 was waiting on the tarmac ready to go. Then a familiar face appeared, the Intelligence Officer from Moengo and he immediately put a stop to the argument. He said we could watch the news and forget the plane for now, as I said, weird.

We sat there quiet for a while waiting and wondering why, then it was clear, as the main story of the day, was *us*. It showed us being bundled into the cop shop, then some old footage of John and the previous team from '86.

Then the biggie, John's mutilated body was shown being dragged from a truck in Paramaribo. Bill, again translating, told us the story. Apparently, after an epic battle in Moengo with John and his team (the pretend one, when we dived into the ditch), the JC had bravely killed John and sent the others running for home. They had provided justice for the families of the soldiers that had been killed and now there would be continuing dialogue for peace in Suriname.

I know I am writing this, but you just couldn't write this shit. I looked to the intelligence officer who was watching from the back and I could almost see the promotion written on his face.

Now we had to go quick, so we picked up our belongings and as we jumped into the van some paperwork that we were made to do earlier, was thrust into our hands (our deportation papers), then we sped off, blue lights flashing. We headed to the airport, then bypassed customs and straight onto the airfield through the perimeter fence. It was dark by now and we could see the 747 sat there lit up, engines on tick-over. We abruptly pulled up to the stairs, where there was a stewardess waiting at the top. As we got out I could see a mass of faces, all looking through the windows at us. Then all the cops shook our hands and told us to go quick.

We didn't need telling twice, so we grabbed our kit and legged it up the stairs as fast as we could. As we stepped on board, immediately feeling the cool air of the air conditioning, one of the air hostesses quickly closed the door behind us (apparently it had been waiting a long time).

Then as another stewardess took us to our seat's I could see that all the passengers, who were now all staring at us, had been moved to either the front or the back of the plane and there was a large gap of empty seats all around us. We quickly put our kit in the overheads and sat back down as the plane was moving off.

Strange to say now, but I still wasn't sure whether we were out of trouble yet and listened intently for the voice on the speaker. It came in French, but I understood perfectly that this plane was now on route, directly to Paris and not Paramaribo. I looked at the boys who were thinking the same thing, relief in all our faces.

After the plane took off and finally got to altitude, the very attractive air stewardess who seemed to have been solely assigned to us, came over and poured us all a drink. Al then said, "I wonder if she has some Nutella." That was it, we all lost it big time and snot and drink went everywhere, but after a stern look from the big chief lady at the front of the plane, we sat back quietly, doing as we were told.

Everything over the last few weeks had seemed to have moved at a hundred miles an hour, I still find it exhausting thinking about it, even now. I hoped the journey might give me some time to what they call now, decompress and as we flew on through the night, I couldn't help smiling to myself.

I thought about the intelligence officers, both now sitting behind much bigger desks, Joseph, in some Ambassadors mansion, discussing the fate of some other poor unfortunate, running his hand across his throat and Ronnie, sat at the negotiating table at the UN with his shiny pistol on the table.

Then back to us, randomly picked, as scape goats, as John had no intention and as I knew now, not even the means of paying us the £30,000 promised. I momentarily questioned where I would go from here, and what would happen when we got back. But I realised that right now, none of it really mattered, I was alive and going home, that is what I needed to focus on and be happy with. So, after another large whisky, from Frenchy, I sat back in my seat and fell asleep.

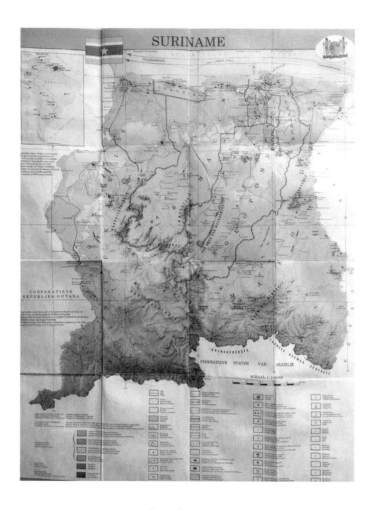

Overview Map.

Chapter 9

Paris/London, 14 December 1989

The 747 touched down at Charles De Gaulle airport, in the early morning of the next day. As we stepped out in our lightweight clothing, the cold cut right through. We quickly made our way across the tarmac (very few airbridges then) and onto passport control, just waiting to be stopped with a hand on the shoulder or an 'Excuse me, sir'.

Nothing happened. We went through without any confrontation, then carried on through the terminal, somewhat perplexed about what to do next, since we were sure we'd be marched, by the authorities straight onto the next plane to Heathrow.

Bill looked at our deportation papers again. It said nothing about where we were actually to be deported to.

"Fuck!" said Al. "This means we'll have to buy our own tickets back to Blighty!"

So, after rummaging through our bags of money and pulling out some French Francs, we went to the BA desk to do just that.

As we sat waiting in the departure lounge, looking a bit dishevelled, we went through every possible scenario for when we got to the UK.

"Well, nobody's batted an eyelash so far," shrugged Bill. "Maybe it'll be okay."

"Yeah," Al agreed. "Given what's happened up to now, hopefully they'll let us just slip back into the country, without any shit."

While we talked, the back of my neck prickled and I gazed around, scanning the crowds. I couldn't help feeling that although we had not been intercepted by the French, we still were being watched.

The flight home was quick and after picking up our bags from the carousel, we went to passport control. There was the same lack of interception, but I was aware that the UK's intelligence community knew exactly who we were and where we were.

As we sat in the taxi that would take us home, and as we had, put our larger back packs through check in, we checked that all of the money and the gold were still in our kit. There was visible relief when we established that it was.

As I looked out of the window of the cab and caught sight of the various landmarks of London flashing past, I began to relax a little. I knew it would come, but it seemed that I had a little breathing space.

I was the last to be dropped off. I looked up at the building, depressed by the grey miserable surroundings and the thought of going into the glorified bedsit I was still renting. Already I was getting a rose-tinted view of where I had just been.

I got in, made a cup of tea with rat pack (British Field Rations) milk and switched on the telly, looking for the news to find out what had been happening back in the UK. As always, it was the same regurgitated shit, but I was still a little worried that we might pop up in the foreign news section.

Thankfully, we did not. As I sat there drinking my disgusting tea, I tried to figure out what to do next.

It was only then, that I began to come to grips with the enormity of what had happened over the last few months.

First, I considered the random selection of us all, by John. And his complete lack of any understanding – not just of soldiering, but of how the world turned. Did he really think he could just blag his way through, taking money from everywhere and not delivering? Then, trying to play both sides! Could he have really not expected anyone from the security services to notice? It absolutely beggared belief to think that somehow, through a completely random act, this complete arsehole was put in a position of authority! Eventually, it could have only ever gone one way, with someone like that.

After his death, when we gradually pieced together what he had done, I began to feel glad that I had been there, to watch the lights go out in his eyes.

Then, there was the politics of war. As a soldier, things are pretty straightforward – you get your orders and you act on them. However, for us, any sort of structured orders process had gone completely out of the window. We just had to act whenever needed, trying to get to grips with constantly changing circumstances. They talk about the fog of war!

In that short period of time, I had watched, listened and adapted very quickly to the shit that was happening around me. Without any sort of top cover, I had made myself useful. Even with the everyday threat of death, I had facilitated what the powers that be, ultimately wanted. I had also seen the dark underbelly of life and was beginning to understand how the world actually worked.

With all this, I came to understand that I would now, never again be 'just a soldier'. I thought about which path I was going to go down. But the answer was now no longer in my hands. With my head bursting, I went to bed and tried – but failed – to get some sleep.

The next morning, the phone rang and I opened my eyes to see daylight just beginning to filter through the grubby blinds. I looked at the clock, which said: 08.30. Still worn out from the journey, I staggered to the phone, expecting it to be Al.

"Alright, mate?" I yawned.

I went silent, hearing the voice of the man at the other end, call my name. My ears were buzzing and I missed the first things he said by way of introduction.

He went on: "An officer from Special Branch will be over to pick you up in one hour's time. Make sure you bring all the information and any photographs you have of your time out of country with you." He paused, but I remained speechless, my head whirling. "Do you understand?"

I replied with a simple "Yes." The phone clicked off.

As I raced around the flat getting ready, I tried to anticipate any questions they might ask me. I remembered the meeting in the YMCA and thought about me discussing the fate of John's team – all the time knowing again, that with these people, any bullshit wouldn't work.

I looked at myself in the mirror: tanned, cleanshaven and a little slimmer than a few months before. I had put on some respectable clothes: of a pure wool sports jacket, a dark polo-neck jumper and chinos – a uniform out of uniform – that I wore with those I bodyguarded.

Then the intercom buzzed and when I answered, a voice reverberated, "The car is waiting."

I quickly checked myself again, grabbed the bag in which I had packed all the requested information, then headed down the stairs and outside into the wintery air.

The Special Branch officer, was standing there with the car door open. He was dressed in a very nice suit and looked as if he could handle himself, even with a bit of a belly. He was also carrying. I noticed the bulge under his jacket and the way he held onto the bottom hem in the wind was a giveaway. He told me (in a way that got my back up a little), to get into the back of a very large maroon coloured Rover. So, trying to keep the upper hand, I asked for his warrant card. After I had watched him squirm a bit, as he tried to get it out and still keep his gun concealed. I jumped in and we sped off. As one of those who probably had a get out of jail free card, he didn't hang about and with me hanging onto the door handle for most of the journey, we were soon in the centre of London.

The car stopped and I was ushered into an old building that had the number 53 on a small brass plate in the doorway. The SB guy tapped the intercom, said his surname and the lock buzzed open.

"Get the lift up to the first floor," he told me. "Get out, turn right and go along to the door at the end of the corridor."

He then went back to the car and, after eyeing the mirrored glass of a small booth in the hallway, I did exactly what he said. As I left the lift, I saw that the top of the stairway was barred by a ceiling-height metal turn-style with what looked like a key code entry system. From the ground floor reception, you would never know that, internally, this was a very secure building indeed. Very aware of the security camera, now pointing directly at me, I made my way along the corridor and knocked on the door, my mouth feeling like sandpaper.

A slightly effeminate man's voice – one that I recognised, since I had spoken to him on two separate occasions when the shit was hitting the fan – told me to come in!

Balding, and in his 50s or early 60s, the man sat at a desk to the left of the door, with a large array of filing cabinets opposite him. There was a further door into another room and through its frosted glass, I could see a figure in there.

"Do you have some form of ID?" he asked, which threw me a bit, because he knew who I was. I handed him my MOD 90 (Army ID), which he barely glanced at, before giving it back to me.

Pressing a button on the phone, he said, "He's here."

It was all very 'American TV Private Detective'. Without getting an answer, he gestured to the door and told me to go through.

Upon entering the room, there was the same middle-aged man with greying hair who had caught my eye in the Army Surplus store, back in September. The phone call earlier on, had seemed a little threatening, but now he asked me to sit down, in a manner that seemed friendly enough. I hoped it would stay that way. Again, he didn't say who he was, or which organisation he worked for, but given the manner in which I had first been approached and now had been summoned, he wasn't from the Salvation Army.

As he looked over some paperwork – a standard gesture to demonstrate superiority – he calmly said, "Tell me the whole story. From the moment you were recruited, to your arrival back in the UK."

I took a deep breath and started to relay the whole saga. He only interrupted to clarify who was who and to ask for some rough dates; but apart from that, he let me explain everything. I did realise that I was probably being recorded, so I was very careful in the way I delivered the information, whilst being as honest as I could be.

When I'd finished, he again calmly asked me, "Does that bag contain the information I requested?"

I nodded and laid it out on the table.

I began to remove the items from it. There were the aerial and ground maps of the country I had been working from, all the reels of photos I had in my possession, and the contact information I had taken from John's belongings, immediately after he had been shot dead.

With the maps in front of us, he made me go over it all again, telling him everything in more and more detail (standard FBI). The maps were not marked up at all – since this was a big no-no, according to my training – but I was able to show him the areas we had moved in, reporting what we had been doing there, and what we had seen.

I was just getting to the end when he asked, "What about the drugs?"

I took a moment, then answered, "Exactly, what do you want to know?"

I think he just wanted to see my reaction, because he dismissed the question and moved on to talk about the intelligence officers who were there. He did not so much ask me about what they were doing there, as tell me about the political situation.

"… That area is very sensitive at the moment…"

I knew all that he was telling me, but I listened intently, still keeping in the role of the subservient little soldier boy, playing the game.

After the questions ended, he told me, "I will keep all you have given me. It will be vetted and returned to you at a later date." Looking directly into my eyes, he told me,

"The French and Dutch have been in touch. They are very happy with the outcome. You did very well, considering the position you were in."

I gave him a humble, "Thank you."

"The American DEA [Drug Enforcement Administration] want to speak with you about the drug situation there." He passed me a card. "That's the number of the person to talk to at the US embassy. Call them as soon as possible."

"Of course," I said.

"You are free to leave, now."

I started to get up, then hesitated, and asked, "What about Al and Bill?"

"They have nothing to worry about," he said. "But I suggest you do not mention our meeting." He must have read my mind, because he added, "Don't worry. You will be looked after."

I then stood, picked up my now empty bag, and went to the door. Just as I put my hand on the handle, he called me by my nickname, which unnerved me a little.

As I turned to look at him, he continued, "You can go back to what you did before, but that ultimately is up to your CO. I will just add that – I may need to speak to you again."

There was no answer from me; just a look of acceptance, and I left.

I stepped out of the building, able to breathe freely again, thanking my lucky stars that he wasn't interested in the money we had made, or the gold that we now needed to sell. I looked around, but there was no car waiting for me now. So, putting my collar up against the hideous British winter, I took a final look back at the imposing building, and then unceremoniously made my way to the nearest tube station.

Epilogue

It has been well over 25 years since all this happened and it is only now that any restrictions have lapsed that I am able to talk about it.

To be honest, I probably would never have written this, if it wasn't for a personal and emotional chain of events that seemed to force it out.

A few years before I began to write this, I had what I thought was just a little bit of a midlife crisis. It happened at the age of 48, when I'd almost lost my life on another job. As with everything else that had happened to me, I never spoke to my family about it. But perhaps because I was getting on a bit by then, it must have affected me more than I thought.

I'd always had a really strong bond with both of my children. I still spend a lot of time with my son, who is now an officer in The Royal Airforce – riding our mountain bikes or wringing the life out of my race car on the test track together. However, it's the Dad-daughter thing that really makes you putty in their hands. In my eyes, my daughter could do no wrong and I worshiped her.

Over the next couple of years as she went into her late teens, I thought I was losing her. I know, now, that I was wrong; but at the time, I thought she simply didn't care about me at all. Thinking about all the things I had done, the risks I had taken over the years, coupled with the fact that I had almost been killed again – deep inside, I began to feel angry.

This was completely stupid and selfish, because how the hell were my family to know why I was feeling the way I did, when I had never talked about what I had done with any of them? However, as I felt the apple of my eye was drifting further and further away from me, a darkness was forming.

Then, one night, for no sane reason – I know, now – but angry at her, I grabbed my daughter and threw her out of the house, into the night and into the rain.

I had now not only lost the bond, I had smashed it into a thousand pieces.

I left our family home that night and did not return for over seven months.

My wife, now completely distraught, could not believe what I had done, but she kept her strength and realised that there was something deep within me that I could not control. I have never been a talker. I have had friends for over thirty years who really know nothing at all about me, or what I have done. My wife said I really needed to speak to someone, a professional who dealt with these things.

Let me get this out, first: I do not have PTSD, (post, traumatic stress disorder). As a former qualified adaptive ski instructor, working with the Battle Back program. I had worked very closely with injured people in the military who did have it – and I say again, I do not.

However, as always, my wife was right – I did have a problem with something and I booked some sessions with a counsellor.

For my whole life, I had laughed at people who talked about such things, but as I began to speak openly about my life, the weight of the world I was carrying, now seemed to be easing off my shoulders a little. As I spoke to the counsellor, I realised that what I had been carrying around, was not the kind of thing he was used to hearing. Even though I left out anything security sensitive and kept things very vague, his jaw began to drop and he went into some sort of trance as he sat there, transfixed, listening. I only went to see him a few times, but he was an enormous help and I cannot thank him enough.

One of the things he said could help me, was to write down my real feelings and try to communicate these to my daughter. This I did. But I found that what was creating these feelings, was the fact that she didn't know the real me at all.

As I got help, I began to open up more and more with my wife, which created another reason for my telling this story. My wife said, "You should write about your life, it might help – just putting it all down and getting it off your chest."

Since I didn't know where to start, I asked my daughter, who was still only at the point of tolerating me, to help. She was an English student and already an accomplished writer and budding playwright, at that time. As we sat at my computer, I began with the story of Suriname, warts and all, and, as the days and weeks went on, I hoped she now could understand a little of where the darkness might have come from.

That is where I am now – still writing, and hoping that, one day, my daughter will find it in her heart to truly forgive me, as I don't think I can ever, forgive myself.

After Suriname, I had personally changed beyond recognition. My life also changed dramatically, and I went on to do things that most people could only dream about. The fact that I was able to keep my mouth shut, led to a number of doors opening up for me and I have been careful, not to bite the hand that fed.

There was, however, one little glitch in my attempts to climb the greasy pole of success.

Many years later, after I had become very successful in the area in which I was now working, Mick and Pat had concocted a plan to try to discredit me and my team from Suriname. They had got in touch with a TV reporter called Roger Cook and tried to frame me Al and Bill for the murder of John. That was rich, considering that neither of them where there, and did not have a clue about the knife edge situation we were in. Mick also had taken part in the murder of six men while they were sleeping.

Apart from within the security services, I had never spoken about what Mick did. This, and the fact that I had saved his pathetic life – risking mine on a number of occasions to do so – really tore out my insides. I thought about meeting with the reporter and telling him the real truth about 'Private Pike', but again, I held it all back. I have learned, over the years, that news reporters print the story they want to print, and the truth can be just an inconvenience, that gets in the way.

When Mr Cook did manage to get me on the phone and asked me to tell my side of the story, I told him I would meet in two days' time at a hotel in Newcastle.

Then, I immediately called 53.

They told me to go to the hotel, and from reception, to contact the reporter in his room and get him to come down. Then, I was to leave immediately and they would deal with it.

I had no more calls from Roger Cook.

The programme did come out, but my face was the only one that was never really shown clearly and a few weeks later, Cook was in court on fraud charges. Coincidence?

What made me laugh most was that Mick was interviewed – and he called not just my team, but everyone out there 'cowboys'. "Yeah man. They were all just cowboys."

As with Omleo, what can you say to that?

I never found out what happened to Ped and Gary. I was glad they got back safely, and I hope one day to meet them again and shake their hands, because it is now all water under the bridge.

'Private Pike' became a security guard on a cruise ship. I found out which exact ship from a guy I met years later in North Africa – let's call him 'Thor'. He was a fixer out there and anything you needed – weapons, vehicles, or a helicopter for a fast track out – he was the man. He had previously been one of the SNCOs (senior non, commissioned officers) in Mick's unit and had then gone on to serve with a French SF unit with the acronym CRAP. Yes, we both had a good old laugh at that one! He told me that when more and more Brits joined from the legion, the unit used more the name GCP (Group Commando Parachutists) – thankfully.

Meeting him completely changed the way I looked at Legionaries. We became good drinking buddies and had a good old giggle about 'Colonel Mick'.

Pat 'Gold Medal' Baker went back to mini cabbing in his local area.

Bill, given the new age of technology, went into something that was completely over my head. We still keep in contact once in a blue moon, and I can still sit sponging off his huge brain for hours.

Al's life, believe it or not, became a love story – in another war, in another part of the world. He is now semi-retired from his security contracts in Iraq and Afghanistan; living in Bosnia with his lovely wife and beautiful daughter. We keep in contact regularly and he still is as genuine now as he was back then. The bond between us, as strong as ever. I have had the privilege, to read memoirs of his further adventures, and if they ever do, go to print, stand back Ryan and McNab.

Ronnie is still Ronnie. Look on Wikipedia and you will see that he still lives a very colourful life and is running for Prime Minister of Suriname – despite the fact that both he and Bourtese are wanted for drug-running in several countries.

The world never changes.

As for me? Well, the change of path and the climb of the greasy pole began back in March 1990, when I got a call from a security firm in London. Now, this wasn't one of the Micky Mouse ones I had worked for previously. This one was manned only by very select former SAS, SBS and members of 14 INT [Northern Ireland military intelligence unit]. This was one that did have authorisation to carry firearms on occasion, and it was one of the top firms at the time.

I was told that I had been recommended as someone they could trust, and was offered a job – doing static surveillance on a house in west London. It sounded a bit lame after what I had been through, but I took it. Not because I was impressed by the firm that invited me (I still wanted out of the security circuit) but because I was looking for a foot in the door with the people who had recommended me.

Also, I thought (wrongly), it would be far away from all the Walters reaching for imaginary guns.

Two days later, after a crash course in the tech I was to use and a briefing on what I was actually looking out for, I was now working with the guy who had given me the tech talk, and on a rota with two other teams in a very expensive empty house on The Bolton's, Kensington.

I was told that Madonna had a pad there, but that wasn't the house we were scoping. The house we were interested in, was just along the curved street. We had a very good view of the front and side of that building, from the front bedroom and the roof skylight of the house we now occupied.

The house we had eyes on, was frequented by an Arab, a very important one at the time. It was Saddam Hussain's Foreign Minister and right-hand man, Tariq Aziz.

Then, on the 2nd of August 1990, Saddam Hussain, invaded Kuwait.

About the Author

After being accepted back into the services, the author held a number of different posts. Years later, he was recognised by the queen for, quote: "17 years outstanding military service, as a member of the forces, in the service of Her Majesty the Queen and the country."

After working for a prominent private security company in surveillance, then technical advisor and whilst still a sergeant within the reserve forces, he went on to become an extremely successful film and TV stunt man.

After winning a Hollywood World Stunt Award in 2013 for his in-flight plane-to-plane hijack jump on the Batman film, *Dark Knight Rising*, he has now become a very well-respected stunt coordinator and action unit director.

Along with his many skills, he is an accomplished amateur racing driver, ski and skydive instructor and has represented his country in extreme sports.

When not working on a movie or following his passion as an amateur racing driver, he lives between his homes in the UK and the Spanish Canary Islands, where he continues to write.

Me and Bill in snap ambush position with LMG.

Me and Bill in Moengo.